When women are trying to cope with a problem, struggling through a major life transition, or just in need of a reality check and a little healing support, we go straight to our friends. Each of the books in the *Women Talk About* series reflects the experiences of dozens of women from diverse backgrounds, whose words are accompanied by provocative insights from the latest research. Often funny, sometimes painful, and always honest, their powerful voices reassure us that we're not alone, offer guidance and wisdom, and show us how to connect back to the woman we want to be.

Juicy Tomatoes

Plain truths,
dumb lies, and
sisterly advice about life after 50

Susan Swartz

New Harbinger Publications, Inc.

Publisher's Note

This publication is designed to provide accurate and authoritative information in regard to the subject matter covered. It is sold with the understanding that the publisher is not engaged in rendering psychological, financial, legal, or other professional services. If expert assistance or counseling is needed, the services of a competent professional should be sought.

Distributed in the U.S.A. by Publishers Group West; in Canada by Raincoast Books; in Great Britain by Airlift Book Company, Ltd.; in South Africa by Real Books, Ltd.; in Australia by Boobook; and in New Zealand by Tandem Press.

Cover design by Blue Design
Edited by Angela Watrous
Text design by Michele Waters

Library of Congress Catalog Card Number: 00-134872
ISBN 1-57224-217-5 Paperback

New Harbinger Publications' Web site address: www.newharbinger.com

02   01   00

10   9   8   7   6   5   4   3   2   1

First printing

Dedicated to the memory of Linda Siegfried,
an original tomato.

Contents

Acknowledgments

I want to thank the many women who keep me laughing and thinking. They include my sister and my mother, who taught me about Frey humor, my matchless daughters who keep me honest and tell me when to cut my hair. Plus the writing group, the book group, the Priscilla group, the Gualala group and the Inverness group. I'm forever grateful to my oldest friends who give me their best lines and my newest friends inside this book who took me into their homes and their confidence.

Special thanks to colleague Eileen Clegg who introduced me to New Harbinger and its smart crop of early tomatoes, including wise editor Angela Watrous.,

And, of course, thanks to the big guy.

Introduction

Think about a juicy tomato. The way it feels and smells, soft skinned and absolutely luscious. Perfectly ripe and ready. "Tomato" used to be popular slang for a woman. In old gang ster movies, they'd say something like, "What's a tomato like you doing with these bozos?" And while I normally protest women being compared to inanimate objects, I like the tomato image, it being a fruit, a big ovary really, loaded with seeds.

The fully ripe tomato is not a young, pink, hard-bodied tomato. It has been on the vine for a while, kissed by many suns and washed by many rains. But handled with respect, this saucy creature goes a long way.

This, however, is not a cookbook. This is a book about women who revel in their ripeness from age fifty on. Chronologically they are middle-aged. More important, they are in the middle of life, the thick of it.

Middle age is generally considered to be the age period between forty-five and sixty-five, and while many of us don't feel middle-aged at forty-five, by fifty we get it. Looking at how women age with passion and pizzazz is a favorite focus of mine, ever since that day eight or so years ago when a bunch of my friends and I acknowledged—with some surprise—that we had passed from being young into a new territory.

That getting older can suddenly sneak up on you speaks to our culture's well-honed practice of denial. But we'd have to live in a world without cosmetic commercials, black "Over the Hill" birthday banners, and mirrors to not be aware that "young" is finite.

I wanted to write a book that women can pick up and read on those mornings when they open their eyes and think, "Oh shit, fifty." I have a vested interest in maximizing middle age, which makes *Juicy Tomatoes* one of those "write what you need to know" efforts. When I think about getting older it's not turning a certain number that terrifies me as much as what's associated with it. I don't want to be labeled anything based on my birth date, but we know that happens. There's as much ageism within as without. To fight that we need role models, girlfriends, and others who are our chronological peers to provide new direction, confidence, and commiseration—and to say "get off of yourself" when it's what we need to hear.

The women in this book are not denying the numbers. None of them lie about their age (well, there's this one who when asked her age says, "I'm forty-eight, but I lie"). The important part is they're challenging the old images by what they do and how they think. They're dealing with aging in their own ways. Physically they do it with hormones, plastic surgery, herbs, or no reinforcements at all. But the real adjustment lies in changing the mental and emotional attitude toward aging, and that may call for several assists ranging from antidepressants to a firm talking-to. These women are not "Pollyannas" ignoring the changes that age brings, but they are challenging the cultural belief that getting older is somehow a failure.

We have the numbers to change the image of what fifty is, and we have the motivation. Baby boomers began turning fifty in the late 1990s—one every 7.5 seconds. According to the U.S. Census Bureau, by 2010 the over-fifty population will grow another 30 percent, while the twenty to forty-nine group remains about the same.

The generation that never experienced anything quietly or alone (and is convinced of its singular impact to dictate the rules) is working fast and hard and somewhat selfishly to remodel middle age.

This book is beyond boomers. Those who reached fifty a long time ago and those who will, sooner or later, need reminders that every age is valuable. It's like Abby tells her menopause group, "If we resist being our real age we cheat ourselves of this chapter and our next chapter."

How many women can relate to actor Barbara Hershey, who complained to a reporter how poorly the media deals with middle-aged women and then asked that her age be omitted in the article? Come on, now. Raise your hands. Okay, just roll your eyes. I'll be brave and start. I'm technically not a boomer. The boomer pack is generally defined as people who were born between 1945 and 1960. I was born in 1943, which makes me more of a *sh-boomer* (for those who remember that great doo-wop song by the Crew Cuts). When I'm feeling defensive about my age I point out that it is out of my control. I had nothing to do with when my parents decided to have me. Yet I often feel like I should apologize for not being younger.

It is like a woman in the book *Goodbye Good Girl* says: "Women feel like we've done something bad by growing older" (82).

Goodbye Good Girl, which I coauthored with Eileen Clegg, has a section on aging called "When the Sweet Young Thing Ripens." We included aging as part of the good girl syndrome because the good girl feels guilty for doing anything unpopular—and getting older is definitely unpopular.

As we hit fifty, we want to change all of those negative attributes to middle age, but we can't do that by simply protesting that they're unfair. We need persuasive examples that getting older is okay, something we can handle, something even to look forward to.

Antiaging is not the answer. There are ways today to defy age, as they say in the cosmetic ads, but moisturizers can only do so much. Same goes for cosmetic surgery, because eventually you run out of things to tuck. If we accept getting older, we can relish being mature. We can stop saying, "I'm not ready to grow up," which may sound girlish on someone who is approaching thirty but is really pushing it at fifty.

I once interviewed a female therapist who said that all society wants from the middle-aged woman is a mother who listens. Well, that's very nice, but what about the middle-aged woman who is writing her first short story, running for office, or taking off for Baja because she always had a yearning. And what if she's also dealing with hot flashes, dying parents, and some weird thing going on with her skin.

Getting older is more than menopause and going on your first cruise. It's getting loud and strong and knowing who you are. Curiosity and experimenting never stop. Nor does taking up Tai Chi or moving to Hawaii because there's more hours to surf.

It's easier to be middle-aged when just about everyone you know is, too. Even better if they're managing it with style and humor. That doesn't eliminate some of the real and distressing parts, including the mad-dog blues during menopause (for which PMS is a mere dress rehearsal).

There are some things we all have to deal with. Millions of women are going into menopause every decade, and still the medical experts don't know how to advise us on it. There are other truths about middle age. If you've put off having children, you better hurry up or hope science does. If you had kids in your twenties, they're probably leaving, establishing their own adult lives. There are a lot of people, including your dentist and maybe even your boss, who are younger than you and have authority over you. Parents become dependent and die. It's not easy being a fifty-five-year-old orphan and becoming the family matriarch. Our contemporaries die, too. At middle age you don't jump out of bed quite as fast—or into it, for that matter. And while there are options as to what comes next in life, they may be fewer.

If you're a juicy tomato, or perhaps already sun-dried, I think you will find some friends and role models in here. These women have humor and drama in their lives. They don't make saggy breast jokes, nor do they deny that there are things happening to them that are specific to the un-young. Many of them dragged themselves kicking and screaming over the line into middle age. Some will tell you forty was worse than fifty and that sixty gives them a stomachache. But take heart, because there is a ninety-four-year-old woman in here who says, "This is the best part so far."

So many of the women I met in writing this book sent me soaring. I would walk out of their living rooms and think, "What a great club I get to be in." Their stories and attitudes show more than I can explain about courage, grace, and vibrancy. They're a wide range of no-apologies women who live in different regions of the country and represent varied cultures and lifestyles. I've used first names because it's friendlier, but mostly because I wanted this book to be as frank-talking as possible on everything from sexual appetites to bag lady worries—and for that you need some anonymity.

Like the other books in the "Women Talk About" series, this one has a girlfriends' conversational style and lots of advice from the hot tub. We're going through a lot together. One morning I heard a woman on public radio talking up crone circles, and when I got to aerobics my teacher was asking the class for hints on turning forty-five: Should she dye her hair taxi-cab yellow or get her navel pierced?

A fifty-year-old woman can expect to live at least one-third of her life after menopause. We don't want to deny that gift by regretting and apologizing for being the age we are. Not when we can be passionate, adventurous, vivacious, and sexy. Not when we're finally getting over our fear of heights. We just need to be honest and speak out. When so many women are dealing with transition intelligently and with laughter, the very least that can happen is social change.

Come with me now and enter the world of bone scans and under-the-wire pregnancies. Hot flashes and hot dates. And don't forget running off to Italy—or just walking out on the front porch and looking to see what's coming down the road.

1

What Is Middle Age Anyway?

My moment of truth was when I showed my second husband a photograph of me taken by my first husband and he said, "Who's that?"

—Diane

Things hurt where I didn't know I had things. I know I have more years behind me than I have left in front of me—unless I get to live to one hundred twelve.

—Jan

I don't want to someday become seventy and think I lost twenty years feeling bad. I would really be mad at myself.

—Marilyn

Maybe if you weren't into the counterculture in your youth you don't get as upset about getting older, but we made such a big thing out of being young. I want it to be 1968 and I'm twenty.

—Mary

It Depends on Who's Counting

Fifty is decidedly middle-aged. The dictionary says that middle-age is between youth and old age and commonly thought to be the years between forty-five and sixty-five. Some would start middle age at forty and some would stretch it to seventy. Around forty-five you start thinking that middle age may be something that could possibly apply to you. But it often isn't until our fiftieth birthday that we start to admit once and for all that chronological youth has passed.

Lucy, who had a baby at fifty-four, says: "I guess middle age is between midforties and midsixties. I guess, too, it depends on where I am. Every decade you asked me I'd probably give a different answer."

You may speed off on roller blades in the manner of the young, but fifty is not chronologically young. No way, no how. But it is also not old. It is in the middle. The middle of life. Not over or under the hill, but on top of the hill, or at least high up enough that you can see still more hills.

This is a great time in the history of womankind to be middle-aged, because there are so many of us. Mary, a lawyer, takes comfort in being in a swarm of women dealing with the same issues: "I like going to conferences where the speakers are all about my age, because they're constantly taking their glasses on and off and stopping in midsentence to say, 'Now, where was I?'"

We are a very large, noisy, and belligerent group, middle-aged women being the fastest-growing segment of the population, according to the U.S. Census Bureau. Everyone is studying us. They want to know about our sex lives. They want us to buy their cereal and go to their spas. Attention is finally being paid. At the turn of the twenty-first century, some 30 percent of all adult American women were age fifty or over. That's a lot of people who now think of their fortieth birthday nostalgically.

The spin doctors are helping provide new encouraging words about middle age. Fifty is not what it used to be, they tell us. After all, a century ago many fifty-year-olds didn't have teeth—and they were practically dead. At the beginning of the twentieth century the life expectancy of American women was fifty-one years. And yet some women knew better even back then. According to Kathleen Barry's biography, Elizabeth Cady Stanton wrote Susan B. Anthony to keep plugging away in the struggle to give women the right to vote: "We shall not be in our prime until we're fifty. Then we shall be good for another twenty years at least." Barry notes that the two actually had forty more years together.

At the beginning of the twenty-first century census figures put life expectancy for American women at seventy-nine. There's even something for procrastinators, those wanting to put off milestone numbers as long as possible. Older people think of themselves as fifteen years younger than they are, say researchers. Future-trend writer Faith Popcorn talks in her book *Clicking* about the "down-aging of America," where sixty feels like forty-five and fifty feels like thirty-five. Fifty-four is the average age that women consider the end of youth, according to *Health* magazine. Kate says it's all relative:

> *After I turned fifty I suddenly didn't mind the term "middle age" any longer. In fact, I'm willing to stay middle age forever now because old has an even worse stereotype.*

If boomers have anything to say, by the time they start breathing down sixty-five, they'll kick middle age up to seventy and call it upper-middle age. It's time to rethink numbers, anyhow. More than a century ago Germany's Otto Von Bismarck came up with age sixty-five as the qualifying marker for Europe's first pension plan, but that was in the 1880s, when life expectancy was only forty-five, and sixty-five was way beyond old.

Our increased longevity is naturally going to move what's considered the middle around. Some optimists, like Ken Dycthwald, author of *Age Wave*, predict that late adulthood will soon be postponed from sixty to seventy-five, and old age won't start until eighty or eighty-five.

In the meantime we're still dealing with the old numbers. To apply for Medicare you have to be sixty-five. To take early retirement at some places, fifty-five. To be protected against age discrimination, only forty. And no matter when it officially starts or end, it's still a hurdle to become a middle-aged woman. For many of us it's a chill, a shock, something we'd just as soon put off as long as possible.

On the other hand, Leigh enjoys the mixed messages she sends people who can't typecast her by age:

> *When I hit fifty-nine I tried parasailing. I loved it. I'm the age where I'm supposed to be laboring in hidden places, but I found I love heights. I once read that loving high places is a sign of extreme ego and the need to have power. I also love that I can get away with speeding sometimes because of my gray hair.*

We've got more encouragement than there's ever been to make middle age a positive experience, but Robin says there's still something that whispers to her in the night:

> *You're not as hot as you used to be. No one will want you. You will never pass as young again.*

That comes from our own ageism and it runs deep. Women, more than men, feel restricted by certain expectations and stereotypes attached to certain ages, a lot having to do with stereotypes based on old thinking and stubborn sexism. Once upon a time a woman had singular value. Children and family were her mission in life and her main job. Her physicality enabled her to lure a man and make babies with him, but after that, when those early looks went, what did she have to offer outside the home? It didn't matter that her mind and body continued to work once her ovaries stopped. Fie on that, we say.

They're Talking about Us

A MacArthur Foundation report on midlife at the end of the nineties told us we're actually happier than we thought about getting older, that middle age for most Americans is a period of calm. Apparently we have a greater sense of physical, emotional, and mental well-being than anyone ever anticipated.

Betty Friedan wrote in *The Fountain of Age* that the mental health of women in their fifties is as good as or better than women in their twenties and thirties. She exhorts women to get past the idea that there is any kind of stopping point, menopause or otherwise. At a book signing for her biography *Life So Far*, I asked her what impact feminists are having on the aging process, and she said we are "transforming it": "It used to be thought that women of a certain age had a conservative, dampening effect on society, but women today who have been formed by this tumultous era [of women's liberation] are not going gently into the good night. Over the next decade we will create a whole new image of age." Many women claim sex becomes more satisfying than ever at age fifty, according to Linda Ojeda in her book *Menopause Without Medicine.* Compare that to the old prevailing thought that women automatically turn asexual at menopause.

But that still doesn't make us young. We've changed. There are obvious signs and the first ones are physical, and we're not the only ones who see them. At middle age we will likely not be asked for proof of age to buy Scotch, except for the rare few like Jane, who has her mother's good bones and only a few gray hairs and who was carded at a bar in Key West at age forty-nine. Long-time friends contend that is because she never went out without a hat, even when she lived at the beach in her twenties. She'd sit in the sand all afternoon draped and covered, looking like everyone's nanny. But now Jane is having the last laugh.

Around the age of forty-eight comes an invitation for membership to AARP (the largest senior organization in the country), which shows up in your mail like some long-ignored parking ticket that you've blown off and has now quadrupled. There must be a mistake, you protest, tearing it in little pieces. You can keep ripping them up as they keep coming, saying you'd rather pay full price at a motel than show some clerk your AARP senior discount card. But this is just the first of regular reminders that you have crossed over. If they found you, imagine all the other computers where your birth date is flashing up. Now here comes the Social Security Administration writing to inform you how much money you can expect to live on after you retire.

Then there are the personal moments. Marylu noticed a group of young men looking her way:

My first thought was maybe I should be
concerned they were going to try and mug me.
Then one of them shouted, "You sure are looking
good in your old age." I was forty-eight at the

time. I was slightly insulted, but I said, "Thanks.
I guess."

There are the things that only you notice. Sara talks about looking at this year's holiday photograph against the one five years before, the one she hated because she needed a haircut, and noticing the difference.

It's not bad, but things are changing and they
will not change back. I'm probably looking as
young now as I'm ever going to. Someone told
me I reminded them of Gloria Steinem and I was
flattered, of course, because the woman's
brilliant—but later all I could think of was that
Gloria is fourteen years older than me.

That's not supposed to bother us. We're feminists. We've fought for years to insist that women be measured by more than their looks. But we have our insecure moments. Rachel wails: "Suddenly I'm making appointments to fix my eyes and my feet and noticing that all the other parents at my kids' preschool are much younger than me." Diane reports: "My moment of truth was when I showed my second husband a photograph of me taken by my first husband and he said, 'Who's that?'"

After reading a story by Colette where the middle-aged woman remarks on her fattened wrists, Maureen sighed: "I was watching out for the jaw, the upper arms, the tits, the ass. I didn't know I was supposed to worry about my wrists."

While you used to come home, strip down, and walk around in your underwear, you now come home and rip off your underwear with relief: "Driving home from work I am already out of my bra," says Gretchen.

You may let up on your own rules, traveling in sweatpants and tennis shoes even in business class. You fanaticize about becoming an eccentric. You notice that your friends start to pamper their feet and use the word "orthotics." It is not just your hands that look like your mother's. It is your neck.

You may finally be pleased with your small breasts because you will never have the Queen Mum look now worn by your full-breasted friends. And then you notice your breasts are bigger and lower. Your eye doctor mentions bifocals and you think it's a joke even though it's been a long time since you could read both a price tag and an offramp sign.

You make jokes about hot flashes, thinking you are either going into menopause or developing malaria. Your doctor declares that you are well within the time period for beginning menopause, and you realize you were kind of hoping for malaria.

The first thing Rachel wants to know about each new blockbuster author or the next Pulitzer Prize winner is her age: "I need to know how much time I have." She does a lot of age comparing:

> *I study women in the locker room at the health club the same way I used to in junior high gym class. I am not looking for competition. I am looking for confirmation. But I sometimes wonder if the younger women are looking at me and thinking, "Yikes. When does that start to happen?"*

You start having that first discussion with friends about what you would do if you ever thought about having cosmetic surgery, even if you agree you probably wouldn't. Penelope met a plastic surgeon at a party: "He told me, 'I can fix that line between your eyes.' And I hadn't even noticed that line between my eyes."

You begin to really appreciate name tags and actually wish they were required for every large gathering. You remember to do your kegels and you remember why. Your hair gets thinner, all over. There is definite upperarm awareness.

More Than Fleshy Differences

Some changes are much deeper. And quite welcome. You may finally take tango lessons or conversational Italian and not worry about making a fool of yourself. You ask for, and get, a skateboard for your fiftieth birthday. You feel less inhibited about sex than ever before. More sensuous, in fact, about everything, from the morning light to the curve in your partner's calf muscle. You find it easier to apologize, but you also don't take as much guff. Jane declares, "There's a woman at work who has always treated me shabbily no matter how nice I am to her. I've decided that bitch is dead."

You don't feel as self-conscious as you used to, like everyone is watching. You can sit in a restaurant, even a bar, alone, without pretending that you're waiting for someone. Sedonia noticed a new freedom: "I feel freer to be myself, to say what I want to say. I don't care as much what people think. I could tell that something changed inside me."

Adina says she doesn't take herself as seriously as when she was younger:

> I'm not as wrapped up in my little drama. I feel
> settled—not in a sleepy way, but in a rested way.
> I enjoy people much more than I used to. I like
> learning about them. I'm a good listener. I used
> to behave in certain ways just so that I would be

accepted, so I would be loved. I was putting myself in a box all the time. Not now.

Kate says she's a better stepmother:

As I get older I feel more generous and accepting of people who I used to think were put on the planet just to torment me. I also don't hold back on complimenting people, because I've learned how much we need to hear praise and encouragement from others about our work, how we're raising our kids. It costs nothing to tell someone they're doing a good job.

Diana says she lets her "new woman" rip:

I'm outrageous. I laugh out loud. I cry when I want.

Jan sees the good and the bad parts of getting older:

I feel at ease with myself and who I am, but I worry more about my health. Is my heart okay? What's my sugar level? My cholesterol? I chew around my nails while waiting for the pap test and mammogram results. Riding my horse is a little tougher, throwing the saddle on, cleaning the stalls every day. Things hurt where I didn't know I had things. I know I have more years behind me than I have left in front of me—unless I get to live to one hundred twelve.

At midlife there are definite reminders that we are probably not going to live to one hundred twelve. When Sukie found out she had kidney disease and needed a transplant, she described her first experience with a life-threatening condition as "a death of an inner kind. It was the death of a kind of innocence about personal, physical disaster."

After fifty comes a sense of urgency to realign our patterns or correct some things. Mary says she always wanted to believe she was in a dress rehearsal for life:

> *But now I know it's not. It troubles me that*
> *some issues have not been resolved, like what I*
> *want to do when I grow up, should I try to*
> *improve my marriage, will I ever find my creative*
> *self. I still don't like my furniture.*

By fifty we've learned to look to our peers for solace and direction. We often find ways to work the pros and cons of hormone therapy into the conversation. We likely find ourselves speaking unabashedly to other women about the most intimate subjects.

Penelope tells of how much fun she's having:

> *Even though I weigh more than I ever have. Even*
> *though I'm in love with a man I know will*
> *eventually leave me because he wants children*
> *and I don't. After years of advising farm workers,*
> *I've become a prize-winning poet. I love my life.*
> *I laugh at myself now for ever worrying that*
> *after forty life would be linear progress to vaginal*
> *dryness and the grave.*

Are We in Denial Yet?

So, why not just own your age, wrapping it around your neck like a red scarf and walking down the sidewalk with your head high? Because, despite joyful notes about America becoming a gerentocracy full of "new old," it is still, in most people's minds, the nation of youth (even though the numbers prove otherwise). We speak adoringly and even wistfully of young talent, youthful energy, budding beauty. Telling an older person they look younger may sound like a compliment, but maybe it's really a confirmation that young is inherently better.

We love the fine worn wood on our grandmother's piano, but we're not too sure we want to inherit her own fine worn exterior. We collude in our own devaluation.

And that makes us grumpy, resentful, worried, and a little bit ashamed, but there's ageism out there, honey. We panic. We lie. Or we think about lying. The old admonition to never ask a woman her age is tantamount to saying that to reveal it would be embarrassing or that she'd probably lie anyhow, for the same reason. The implication is that lying is a silly thing but probably a damned good idea.

However, Kathleen, a museum consultant, songwriter, and tap dancer, has decided to liberate herself and go for honesty:

> *My old boss warned me once that a woman who tells her age will tell anything, and she meant that in a negative way. But I've turned that around, reframed the sucker, and I say that a woman who tells the truth about her age will tell the truth about everything.*

Sue, on the other hand, didn't want anyone in her office knowing her true age, so the summer her daughter worked at her company, Sue made her daughter promise not to tell her age, either:

> *If they knew she was twenty-eight they'd mentally figure I was a lot older than I let them believe. I think it changes people's perceptions when they know your age. You tell people your age and they'll think, "Hey, now that I look at her she*

*does have those wrinkles." My mother never told
her age or her weight. She told me that people
would use it against you. Besides, she said it was
rude to ask, like asking someone's salary.*

*You can't trust people. If they know your age
they'll make a judgment. In my organization,
when I'm preparing biographical material for an
employee, I purposely delete graduation dates.
That someone has an MBA from Harvard is
relevant. When they got it is not. I never tell any
man I'm going out with my true age, and once
when a doctor asked me I almost thought about
lying to him, too.*

When Jane hit forty-eight she decided to go on hold:

*Partly it was because I look younger than that
anyway, and I also didn't want to be fifty. Then
a story on my promotion that included my age
ran in the newspaper, which forced me to take a
new stance. Now when people ask my age I say,
"I'm forty-eight. But I lie."*

Mary's favorite aunt, who she describes as "energetic,
funny, and cool," religiously lied about her age, taking ten
years off, even to employers:

*It helped that she had children who weren't very
curious and didn't wonder why she was only
fifty-five and getting Medicare. When I turned
fifty I told myself that I was really forty, and
that made me happy all day. I never thought that
my age bothered me, but apparently it does.*

Ageism exists, but maybe the way to fight it is the same
way we fight every other prejudice. We call people on it. We
make a stink. We bring it out into the open. Marianne is a

college English instructor who took her story to her local newspaper, claiming age discrimination. She was fifty-seven:

> *I think there is a fear of older women having power and being challenging. I also think that visually we are an affront to some men. They don't like our physiology, because it is a reminder of their own aging. I was happy to learn that not everyone thought that way. After the story came out a number of my colleagues and students told me they appreciate my experience. When we get older we know more. There are few subjects in my class that I can't address experientially and anecdotally. I was a hippie. I met Eleanor Roosevelt when I was a little girl. If I denied my age I wouldn't have the stories to tell.*

Look at Me, I'm Fifty

Not everyone's hiding their age. Some boomers show flagrant disregard for number phobia and actually celebrate their milestone years. Photographer Adele took herself to Paris on her fiftieth birthday:

> *It was a coming-of-age time and Paris is my favorite place. I wanted a trip where I could just take photos, get up when I wanted to, not work if I didn't want to, and feel completely free. I'd been a parent for seven years by then and my father had recently died. It was the first time I could go away and feel no responsibility to anyone else.*

Lulu's friend gave her Rolling Stone concert tickets on her fiftieth. Lulu's sort of a Stones groupie, even flying to

Europe just to see them perform: "They're my age and I love that they just keep going. Plus, Mick Jagger turns me on." Kate laughs about how she wanted aging to be:

*We want someone to open the door to midlife
and say, "Welcome to fifty. It's zany. It's wild.
It's not at all like you worried about. You get to
wear terrific earrings and everyone thinks you're
very wise, and when they say you're looking good
they're thinking Jacqueline Bisset." That's not
exactly how it happens, but it's worse if you
deny it and hope no one will notice. Then you
miss the good parts.*

Narrow-Minded, Stodgy, Hates Loud Music

There's so much finicky old baggage hanging onto middle age. Middle age spread. Middle age decline. Dowdy middle-aged woman. Predictable. Picky. Set in her ways. Wears an old cardigan over her shoulders and complains about the temperature. Abysmally uncool. Hates loud music, calls the cops when the teenagers next door have parties.

But that's not Jill:

*I was scared of thirty. Forty was okay, but I
needed friends around to make me feel better. At
fifty I felt I was very lucky to be where I was in
life, and I had a great sense of freedom. What's
nice is that I always felt I had to be a certain
way, from adolescence on, and I never was. But
now I feel free to be me more. I don't have to
be young and pretty. I don't have to date. I'm far
less inhibited and I'm much braver. I'm doing*

more now than when I was in my thirties. Now
I want to mountain climb.

So, we change the adjectives. We talk about ripe, full
middle age. Outspoken, unpredictable middle age. We avoid
the cliches and describe the midlife woman as intelligent or
savvy or passionate. How about confident, assured? How
about sexy? We'll take sexy. Sexy as in enchanting. Someone
who enchants with wit and charm as well as looks. Sexy as in
curious, energetic, tempting, alluring, mysterious. Aileen says:

No, we're not young and tight. We're soft and
luscious. I love it. I think our generation
recognizes that in ourselves and sees it in our
friends.

Carolina, who runs a women's bookstore, says her personal mission is to get rid of the word ma'am:

I work with a lot of young people who started
calling me "ma'am." I say you can call me "Doll
face" or "Gorgeous," but don't call me "ma'am."
"Young lady" works too, depending on who says
it. If some sales rep comes into my store and he's
kind of hip looking and he gives me a smile and
says "Hello, young lady," I'm his. "Tomato"?
Absolutely. I know some people use "ma'am" out
of respect, but I say no, call me "Duchess." I
give this lecture to every clerk in the grocery
store. I know your intentions are good, but I
don't want to hear it. How about "Hot Lips"?

Ageism can be lurking in our own old bones. Goldy and
her partner planned a trip to France where they would join a
group of women for two weeks to share a house and paint in
the countryside. At the last minute she had qualms:

*We started to worry that a group of middle-aged
women wouldn't be much fun, even though they
were the same age as we are. When we got there
we found out some of them worried about the
same thing. Of course, it was wonderful.
Everyone was there to have a good time.*

Try On This Image

After novelist Alice Adams died, writer Mary Gaitskill eulo-
gized her in *Salon* magazine and described watching her walk
down a San Francisco street one night:

*She was about sixty at the time and she was
wearing a skirt that fell an inch or so above her
knees and flat heels without stockings. She looked
a little impatient, a little crabby, and very
elegant. I thought, "Unbelievable. No stockings,
and she's making it work."*

The late Charles McCabe from the *San Francisco
Chronicle* wrote a column about women over forty and "the
value of the fully formed woman":

*Older women have form. Men rather deteriorate
after forty, women grow. . . . This is not to say
that women under forty lack their charms. They,
after all, are what women after forty are made
of.*

That was written in 1980. It's been a long time between
poetic comments about the older woman. How about
"robust"? What is the female equivalent of "virile"? Intrepid.
Radiant. Aileen says:

*I'm not sure everyone in society sees us this way,
but I think a lot of us have come a long way
and we can relish ourselves now. We've earned
our life and our status. Maybe not all of society
is recognizing it, but we are where we are no
matter what society thinks.*

How the Media Sees Us

Mary believes that the media didn't prepare her for a very
good image of her middle-aged self:

*My first image of middle age is a picture of fat
women with gray hair in stretch pants at the
supermarket. It's embarrassing to admit that I
think that way even though I know better.
Another thing I'm ashamed to admit is how much
appearances count to me, even though I don't put
much effort into improving my own. The sixties
and feminism gave me the idea we shouldn't
stress our appearance, but sometimes now I think
that after fifty it is all about appearance. There's
nothing in the media that makes me feel better
about getting older.*

Maybe Mary saw the face cream that promises to act
"like a girdle for your face." The media concentrates on the
appearance and drawbacks of getting older and so we do, too,
says Marylu:

*We can say we shouldn't be concerned about
aging, but we are. We're not sure where we fit in
this culture. Things are happening to our bodies.
We're trying to figure out our identity. We don't*

want to become little old ladies that comedians make jokes about.

Carol takes offense at how the media dismisses her age group: "I don't like the media hypnotizing us that we must be young and extremely thin to be attractive. This is very bad PR for us older, rounder types."

Our bodies seem to be our most common vulnerability. Marilyn, a screenwriter, got rid of the full-length mirrors on her closet doors and blames it on how the media makes her not like herself:

> *The media plays to our fears, not our strengths. If you look at the ads, they're about fixing things that I don't feel I need fixed. They've got the couples dancing on the beach because he's taking Viagra. They've got special herbs we can take for our memories. So the message is you're old, you can't think and you can't have sex. They're reinforcing our worries about ourselves, our poor self-image.*

Sam is a former fashion model and now a business executive:

> *Beauty was really important to me and I've been very aware of the unfixable effects of time. Varicose veins. Fallen breasts. One day my daughter told me I was plucking my eyebrows too much—but I hadn't been plucking them. I went into the store and started looking at the creams. Maybe I should get something for my maturing skin or my hair. There were all these products promising to make me look younger. Then I saw one that said it was for old cuticles. And I thought, "This is all so ridiculous."*

Magazine publishers have only recently begun to seriously court the middle-aged reader. Earlier efforts had failed for lack of advertising, but the growing number of aging boomers (with bucks) has caused an attendant boom in anti-aging products, making middle-aged women a hot market. Some of the attempts were positive. Magazines began to feature models who were obviously over age forty, wearing clothes neither girlish nor matronly, next to stories ranging from how regular intercourse can slow aging to the challenge of second careers. It was a start of some kind of age awareness, but not all women bought it. Leigh, a university professor, scoffs:

> *In spite of the very real gains of the feminist movement, our culture still plays games with us, saying if we do such and so, we'll be better, more glamorous. This sells a lot of books and magazines and expensive face creams by creating anxieties we might not have known we had if we hadn't read about them. My ostrich mentality tries to ignore mass media completely, and that keeps me from becoming angry and from feeling insecure about the inescapable facts of aging.*

Adina, who lived in Europe and Asia until settling in California in her fifties, says:

> *It wasn't until coming to this culture that I ever thought about retirement or health issues, social security, making wills. It's the Western worry, and I think it's mostly to push us to buy things. I read the articles in some of those magazines for people getting older and it makes me want to curl up in a coffin.*

Eve, a sociology professor, has an idea about youth adoration:

> *We've been hung up on youth because for the past half century the baby boomers have been on the youngish side, and as we age, I'm sure a lot of specific institutions—work, health care—will shift their focus to the second half of the life cycle. Whether the popular culture will follow is another question.*

Goldy, now a full-time artist after a long career in advertising, says, good luck to those of us waiting for the media to change focus:

> *Image is what people buy. You can show a product being used by a middle-aged woman, maybe on the heavy side, and the consumer who looks just like her will not relate. She will want to relate to the model who is probably thinner and younger, because that's what she wants to look like.*

Goldy's mother hated getting older and Goldy fights to live her middle years more positively:

> *Intellectually I understand that how I feel about my looks is manipulated by the media, but I still buy into it. I fight those negative feelings, but I do have them nagging at me. My mother's life was about being beautiful, and as she got older she pointed out everything she didn't like on her body. That she was getting fat. That she was growing hair where she didn't want to grow hair. We'd go in a restaurant together and she'd complain that all the men were looking at me instead of her. When I start getting those negative*

thoughts I try to fight it. I'll say oh, who cares.
Or I'll go work on a painting to stop obsessing.
What helps is to go do something nice for
someone. Like bringing chicken soup to my
neighbor or sitting down with a younger artist
and seeing how I can help.

California anchorwoman Ysabel Duron took off her wig to show her short gray hair following chemotherapy for cancer, which revealed she was about ten years older than what viewers might have thought. The response was positive. How nice it was, they said, to have real people on TV.

It's a nervy thing to break the mold, says Jeanne:

To be the first to say no to antiaging serum, go
gray, and tell your age is like being the first one
in junior high to show the hicky on your neck.
Everyone says they'll tell just as soon as you do,
but there's no guarantee you won't be the only
one hanging out there.

Doubts and Understanding

Sometimes it's the very act of surviving that makes getting to a certain age more a reward than a curse. In her autobiography *Don't Block the Blessings*, singer Patti LaBelle talked about how thrilled she was to wake up and be fifty, since her sisters died of cancer in their forties and never got the chance.

Sara said she started to feel old at age forty-seven, when she began to gain weight for no reason and clothes didn't look like they used to on her. Then she got some perspective:

When my daughter had a baby, I felt old in a
lucky way because I've been able to have all
these experiences in my life, now including

grandchildren. Complaints about how I look pale against the pleasure of living. When my grandson got ill and had to have a kidney removed, that made me even more aware of my luck in life and health.

Taking a longer look helps to put aging in its place. That may work faster intellectually than emotionally. When Dee turned sixty she panicked:

I told my daughter I felt as though a snake had just crawled across my feet. She was really surprised and said that didn't sound like me at all. She said I sounded like I was repulsed by myself and that I must have swallowed something really awful from the culture.

That milestone birthday was a great year for Dee. She moved into her dreamhome in the country, started a new business that took off, and reunited with a long-ago boyfriend. There was a lot to hoot and holler about, but the chill was still there.

It's the culture. Kate says:

You will tell yourself that age is irrelevant, and then one day you'll meet your daughter's new boss and he'll swear you look like sisters, and you won't believe him but you'll take the compliment anyhow. You might think to make a point and explain, "Actually I was twenty-seven when I had her, and since she's now twenty-five, that makes me fifty-two." But you get all googly instead and say thank you and go off pleased with yourself. It won't last. Two days later you'll be shopping and the clerk will ask if you want the senior discount and you'll want to shove your

*driver's license under her nose to show that you
have three years left before anyone dare offer you
10 percent off.*

Carol changed her job, residence, and marital status in
her late forties. Happy with all of it, she admits that she
secretly wondered what would be the first sign she was getting older:

*I like to think I'm above these things, but I
figured it would be physical, probably when guys
on the construction crews stopped paying
attention to me. As I drove down the street a
young man waved at me from his car. I thought
to myself, "Well, I guess I haven't lost it after
all." Then he proceeded to point at my door and
mouth that my skirt was caught in it.*

"I don't know where I fit in. Not young. Not old," says
Marilyn. For her fiftieth birthday she got out of town with
her husband. They went on a cruise and ended up being the
youngest people on the boat:

*They were wonderful, mostly in their seventies,
enjoying themselves. That inspired me, but it also
made me think I don't want to someday become
seventy and think I lost twenty years feeling bad.
I would really be mad at myself.*

Mary thinks it's a lingering effect of the sixties that gets
in her way of accepting that people don't see her as young
anymore:

*Maybe if you weren't into the counterculture in
your youth you don't get as upset about getting
older, but we made such a big thing out of being
young. Maybe those of us who thought we would*

never be thirty are more upset about aging. I know I am. I still think of myself as a kid and that I can still start a new career or move or do something new. And now I'm starting to think maybe I cannot. I want it to be 1968 and I'm twenty.

Diana says, "I think we have to be open to what's next instead of focusing on what we've lost." Gloria Steinem admitted to Gail Sheehy in the book *New Passages* that even as a feminist crusader, she, too, had anxiety about getting older. She explained that for a long time aging felt to her like a loss. "Then gradually I began to realize it wasn't a loss—it was another country" (124).

Middle age was literally another country for Judith, an American who moved to Prague. She insists that her fifties have been the best part of her life:

I'm over so much. My sons are raised. I went back to school in my forties. I survived breast cancer. By fifty I had accomplished a lot and was emotionally and psychologically ready to take off for adventure. The best part of living in a foreign city is you never know what's going to be around the corner.

There's no way we can try out everything we want to by the time we're forty-five. Maybe it's too late to become a concert pianist if you've never taken a lesson, but that doesn't mean you can't take it up if you've always wanted to learn. You don't have to look far to find examples of many versions of late bloomers. The writer Penelope Fitzgerald didn't get published until she was close to sixty. Carolyn Heilbrun was sixty-two when she published her book *Writing a Woman's Life*. Georgia O'Keefe moved off into the desert at the same age.

Marylu's goal for herself is to keep moving forward. She teaches, has a private counseling business, and made a promise to herself that when she turned fifty she would start to paint again.

Adina enjoys the freedom to be ambiguous:

> *I am not certain about things like I used to think I had to be. Now I can comfortably say, "Actually, I have no idea." Not needing to know opens up a lot of doors.*

Sedonia is committed to not matching the old image of women being useless after menopause, but she's a realist:

> *We can't say it's just all groovy. There are big down sides. You lose your vision, your beautiful head of hair, your face is not like a peach anymore, you get tired. There's a lot of loss. I miss the energy I had, the way I used to look. But it's a fabulous time to be an older woman, and I wouldn't have said that twenty years ago. Things are changing.*

But What's So Bad about Getting Older?

Is it simply our personal dismay over physical changes that make us dread getting older, or is it also that we'll now be perceived by others as less valuable in our youth-worshipping culture? Where does that worship come from in the first place? And who does it serve? Carol thinks it comes from fear:

> *I think most everything against anything, every "ism," is fear-based. In this case it's the buried*

*fear of becoming old and powerless, and the fear
of dying. I guess if ageism serves anyone it serves
the young, but for them it's only a temporary
benefit, given that age discrimination will
eventually hurt them too.*

Mary blames herself for encouraging the same ageism
that she now feels victimized by:

*Part of the problem is the very real feeling
younger people have that they are smarter and
more hip than older people. As a member of the
sixties generation, I was certainly as guilty as
anyone else. Part of it is the American throwaway
thinking that doesn't respect wisdom and
tradition. I guess if older people valued themselves
more, others would too. I hope all of us baby
boomers who think we are so interesting and so
cool can remember to keep valuing ourselves.
That may change the whole thing.*

Sara says ageism is tied into sexism:

*It's all about power. The basis for a woman's
power historically was her beauty and her youth,
and when that changes she needs another kind of
power. Even men are treated like women when
they get older unless they have the kind of power
our culture respects the most—corporate or
political power, wealth, or stardom.*

Sydney thinks that's starting to change. After a blowup
with her long-time employer, she went looking for a new job
at fifty and worried that her age would be held against her:

*It actually worked in my favor because I had a
scandalous predecessor and they were looking for*

*someone who was solid and settled. I think they
were also delighted that I am a little bit off the
wall. I make my boss, who is in her thirties, look
good. She told someone that she wouldn't have
thought a person of my age would have energy
were it not for knowing me. I also like working
for her because she is more efficient and
professional than some of the bosses I've had who
are my age and older.*

Leigh, however, says she senses some prejudice where
she teaches college:

*I sometimes feel ignored. In my teaching I think
some students tend to regard me with a suspicion
I didn't notice ten years ago. Have they changed
or have I? Or is it simply the increasing
difference in our ages? I truly don't know.*

Jamie thinks there are age lines drawn that encourage
ageism. She personally resents senior discounts:

*You start getting them in your fifties. But if
you're in your fifties why do you need to save
money on the airport shuttle? It says, "Here is
the line, anyone over it is old." That kind of age
definition sets you out of the mainstream, says
you have a special need. I think what ageism
does is makes people feel invisible. If you stop
getting looks because you're not young—and I
don't mean just from men but from all of
society—then it's like people are indifferent to
you. And that is the ultimate isolation. That's
what I don't want to happen to me.*

Barbara was the only African-American in a predominantly white school and grew up having to confront racism. She's not about to be stopped now by ageism:

> *I refuse to be invisible. I look in my mirror and say, "I'm getting better every day, even with this belly. These dimpled legs carried all those babies. I have my big ass and my breasts are sagging. But I'm making more money than I ever did and I'm spending it. My life is much richer and more fulfilling than when I was young. I also think when we're going through menopause we become who we really are, not holding back like we used to feel we had to do. If we're angry, it's because of all the crap we've bought into for twenty-five years. I'm not going to do that anymore. I rejoice that I am my best right now.*

Sophie's a history buff and looks for the roots of the devaluing of older women:

> *I'm sure it's not politically correct, but I do believe we human animals are hardwired to reproduce. Males look for nubile—that is, fertile—females; females look for the guys with the biggest pile of rocks or fish, those best able to support the family. The* Old Testament *has stories about men taking younger second or third or fourth wives to ensure offspring. There was good reason for that when infant mortality was as high as it must have been in those days. Not only did they want to carry on their own families, but the kids were needed as field hands in agricultural societies. So the older, less-fertile wives started to lose their power. I think that still shows up today.*

Susanne thinks ageism is sometimes reinforced by technological changes:

> *The unbelievably speedy, even explosive growth in our scientific world leaves the previous generation behind—"out of it" and seemingly unproductive—particularly if we're not as mesmerized as the younger generation by all of it. Then we are suddenly fuddy-duddies. Of course we can look at the entertainment world and advertising and blame them for focusing only on the young, but I think they are responsive to trends, rather than creating them. After all, they are trying to make money, not be missionaries.*

It's the dread of old age that makes Rachel reluctant to embrace middle age:

> *I see old age as a sad, lonely time when people don't look at you anymore, when people talk down to you. I saw this happen when my father stopped being able to drive and lost his independence. He was the most free, strong, charming, and handsome man, and he lost just about all of that. The memories of his getting sick and dying are so fresh that all of my own signs of age scare the hell out of me. I'm trying to change that and not equate aging with getting sick. I'm trying to turn that around and see the wisdom and experience that also come with being older.*

Myth Busters

There's a certain presence that can be achieved with age. It's called pizzazz, a word which the *New Dictionary of American Slang* suggests comes from "piss and vinegar," and generally stands for energy. It comes across in attitude, a certain way of walking, a display of confidence.

Faye has been a flight attendant for more than thirty years and believes that energy is sexy at any age. Faye has streaked blonde hair, multiple earrings, and a laugh that can be heard from coach to first class:

> *I don't get as many looks as I used to, but I*
> *don't feel any change in how I'm appreciated for*
> *being me. As I get older, that same fun,* bon
> vivant *person I've always been continues, but I*
> *also like to think that I am constantly reinventing*
> *myself. I taught myself to roller blade and then I*
> *signed up for a ropes course, which is supposed*
> *to develop courage and trust and which had me*
> *walking tight-wire fashion between two trees up*
> *sixty feet or something. I was up there and*
> *started swaying back and forth and I told myself*
> *to not look down. My heart was beating so fast.*
> *Then I was walking across and when I got to the*
> *middle I started freaking. I took a Yoga breath*
> *and told myself, "You're doing this. Don't quit." I*
> *like doing things that scare me. I don't think it's*
> *a good idea to stay in your easy spot.*

Faye's plan is to put in a few more years of flying and then quit, get her personal trainer certificate, and hold meditation retreats. She started flying when the job required women to be cute and young, weigh no more than a carry-on, wear silly hats, and suffer the gropes and leers of male passengers who believed "coffee, tea, or me" was a frequent flyer's bonus.

> *When I first started flying they only hired young women. You couldn't be married. After thirty-two you were out. Remember the PSA attendants? They wore hot pants. It was such a sexual image, ignoring the whole fact that the reason we were there was for safety. Now there's a lot of older women flying. I'm fifty-five and I'm only halfway toward the top of the seniority list. But I always get from people, "Are you still flying?" as if I should be doing something different by now. It used to make me feel defensive about staying in the same job, about never finishing college. But my choices have been right for me. My attitude as I get older is that it's more important to be who I am than to worry about what people think I should have done.*

Faye looks forward to one day being the matriarch in her family:

> *I think there's something wonderful about being the wise woman to whom people pay attention and respect. I see that in other countries where there is a strong family structure and where women are revered at all ages. In Brazil whole families go out to dinner and stay out late. Kids, grandparents. They don't separate by generation like we do here. I'd like to have that. I understand not wanting to be stereotyped as old, with the negative parts, but I don't want to deny*

*my age and give up the status that an older
woman can earn in her family. Of course I can
do without the bubble hairdo. And I never want
anybody saying I'm too old to roller blade.*

The Daughters Are Watching

Meanwhile, Faye enjoys observing her college-age daughter in bloom:

*I admire her sense of self and I love watching her
own her beauty. We were walking down the
beach together and I just smiled at how many
people were staring at her as she sailed past them
with her head high. Did I want them to look at
me instead? No. You have a child and she's like
a little bud and then the petals start to open and
you can stand back and say, "We made that." It
is a thrill to be in her presence. But I don't envy
her youth. I want to be a strong example of
what comes next.*

Mary, mother of an adolescent daughter, says we should put photographs on our walls of smart, creative, defiant older women to give our daughters something to look forward to:

*Older women say they feel invisible. We need to
bring them out. Put them on magazine covers.
Write screenplays about them. Take them to
lunch, pour them some good wine, and pick their
brains. Bring them around the house. Elect them
to office. Put them in front of our faces and our
daughters' too.*

A mother-daughter camp-out put together a group of daughters in their twenties and their mothers—women old enough to have daughters in their twenties. Kate says:

> *When you have women of all ages and sizes*
> *stripping down to shorts and T-shirts and then*
> *taking it all off to run into the communal*
> *showers, you break barriers. The younger women*
> *were more apt to jump out of the rafts and bob*
> *along the rapids, and they could certainly get in*
> *and out more ably, but in terms of enthusiasm*
> *and sense of adventure there wasn't much*
> *difference. We had three generations there and we*
> *all looked kind of alike, under our baseball caps*
> *and behind sunglasses. Later my daughter said she*
> *was going to have to rethink her idea of age. She*
> *said, "I think that after midlife the party starts."*

The mother of two daughters, Lily says:

> *I can look at young women now without feeling*
> *the envy I did when I was in my forties. I can*
> *look at their loveliness and enjoy their vibrancy.*
> *Open my heart to them. I think my daughters*
> *don't see me as that much different from them*
> *and we do look alike. But one day we were in*
> *the bathroom talking and I studied my one*
> *daughter's face and eyes for so long that when I*
> *looked back at my face in the mirror I almost*
> *screamed. I thought I was more her face than*
> *mine, but mine's older and I found the difference*
> *shocking.*

Georgie doesn't have children, but a lot of her friends are younger women she met working in a law office. One coworker who is Georgie's contemporary routinely used menopause as an excuse for every bad thing—depression, headaches, gaining weight, all-around grumpiness:

> *She kept telling the younger ones how awful it was to get old, saying, "You just wait and you'll see," in a threatening way, like the witch to Snow White. She actually told them that you automatically lose your stomach muscles after menopause. But you know, the reason she had a big stomach was because she never exercised. After a while I couldn't stand hearing that, so one day I just butted in and said, "I want you to know that it isn't necessarily like that. Menopause has not been a problem for me." I thought her attitude was so off-putting and it just played into the stereotype that youth has it all and we have nothing but complaints.*

Jill, a nurse, says her twenty-seven-year-old daughter, who has a master's degree and an international job, already has begun worrying about looking her age:

> *I tell her she's beautiful and doesn't need to worry, and I know the best thing I can do for her is not to worry about my own aging. I'm a bit of a hypocrite, though, because I love it when people tell me I don't look fifty-seven.*

2

It's Only Skin Deep

I need to do something physical every day to feel good. I think being physically strong makes me determined to not limit myself in other ways.

—Lulu

She had flesh you could dive into. Compared to her, the pared-down exercised people were robots. She was the real human body, the sexiest thing around.

—Grace

I look at my older friends and they are beautiful. The etchings around the eyes. A sculptor couldn't do that.

—Kathleen

I try not to worry about my looks as much anymore. I spent my facelift money on a trip to Turkey and Greece.

—Georgie

Maybe Mother Nature Doesn't Need to Be Defied

The cultural standard for beauty is so limited that we sometimes think there is only one style and type of beauty and it belongs exclusively to a certain age. Once past that age there are only vestiges. "She must have been lovely when she was young," we might say, implying she isn't now. Penelope says about her friend Kaye:

> *When I first met her I would look at her and try to see how she would have looked when she was beautiful. Now I just see her. I had to pierce through that cultural thing that you can only be beautiful when you're young. Kaye is eighty, extremely articulate, and very soulful. She laughs readily. She has wonderful bone structure. She is not holding a lot of care in her face. She's still receiving inspiration and she's acting on it. And that shows.*

Penelope then tried being as generous with herself:

> *I let my new self be seen by two ex-lovers who knew me when I was thin and had the body that they wanted at the time. I felt very comfortable seeing them. Ironically they hadn't gained a pound, but each of them separately told me I look beautiful.*

Why buy the notion that blonde is better than gray? Smooth better than wrinkled? Low-swinging breasts inferior to perky high ones? What is wrong with a round belly?

The cultural ideal of beauty being a "nonthreatening girl's body rather than a woman's body" serves to keep women preoccupied with body hating, says Carol H. Munter in an interview in *Women's Health Advocate*. Munter co-authored the book *When Women Stop Hating Their Bodies* with Jane R. Hirschmann. Munter says that when we complain nonstop about our bodies we perpetuate the belief that the female body is never entirely acceptable and so end up spending all our time trying to change the way we look rather than trying to change the world. "What do you think would happen if all the women in the world suddenly stopped hating their bodies?" she says she often asks audiences, who reply, "We'd have so much energy, we'd take over the world."

Grace observed a full-bodied bartender in Palm Springs who stood out against the superthin clientele:

> She had flesh you could dive into. She was very
> full bodied, the Matisse woman, in an
> off-the-shoulder blouse. Her body was so inviting.
> Part of it was because she had so much vitality
> and confidence. Compared to her, the pared-down
> exercised people were robots. She was the real
> human body, the sexiest thing around.
>
> We should look at these women so full of
> life and want to be them instead of exercising so
> we can get into our tights and spandex. How did
> we come to glorify desiccated bony bodies and
> looking at the real, robust human body with
> horror, something we need to tuck, remove, make
> smaller?

At least we attempt a healthier attitude. We tell ourselves that the lines and marks we wear on our faces and bodies celebrate our years of life. Sophie calls them "badges of experience" and says, "We should be just as proud of them as we were our Girl Scout Explorer badges. They prove we've learned a few things."

Kathleen sometimes sees her former self in her twenty-five-year-old daughter:

> *I'll catch her making some move or looking a*
> *certain way and I'll think, "That was me." But I*
> *like looking at my older friends, too. One thing*
> *our generation is doing is not isolating ourselves*
> *from other ages. We get accustomed to what*
> *different ages can be. I look at my older friends*
> *and they are beautiful. The etchings around the*
> *eyes. A sculptor couldn't do that.*

Diana says it starts with us:

> *We have to start seeing the beauty in older*
> *women. I've started making eye contact with*
> *older women and I always say something*
> *complimentary. Maybe we can't do anything*
> *about the signs of aging, but we don't have to*
> *see them as negative. I think we can be more*
> *generous with our changing bodies when we don't*
> *see them just through men's eyes.*

In her book *The Beauty Myth*, Naomi Wolf writes, "There is nothing wrong with women's faces or bodies that social change won't cure" (227). Wolf says that cellulite used to be just normal adult female flesh until *Vogue* magazine reclassified it as a "condition." Wolf urges us to "await our older faces with anticipation." She says, "We don't need to change our bodies. We need to change the rules."

Do You Believe in Magic?

"We have B.E. in our family," said Susan at a mother-daughter picnic. "Baggy eyes," she explained, taking off her sunglasses to prove it. Another woman held up her spot-free hands to show the effects of a new hand bleaching formula she was trying out. Meanwhile, one picnic table over and proving no age is immune, a group of twenty-somethings listened to an NYU law student talk about the woman in Manhattan who sends her cosmetics by mail to help with her "changing skin."

Lulu, a surfer, has a strong, firm body from sports and exercise, and her face shows a woman who's lived fifty years out in the sun. She religiously works on her body tone, but she says, "You can't do workouts for the face."

Instead, the cosmetics industry offers a great number of potions that are supposed to fix us up. They are called antiaging and antiwrinkle, and the claims are that they will firm and plump and fill and moisten. That is how we know that the media is paying attention to us. It will like us again, but first we have to dewrinkle. Right?

Don't count on it. After fourteen years of being the face for a famous cosmetic line, Isabella Rosellini got fired for turning forty-two and starting to look older—a grown-up, glamorous Isabella, but apparently not good enough to sell face cream. The manufacturer's customers might have questioned what good it does them to pay money for the same antiaging products that couldn't preserve the cameo face of Isabella. But they still kept pushing their potions, as did Isabella, who retaliated by developing her own line of products displayed on models of all ages, including a sixty-seven-year-old.

Everyone's selling antiaging in a jar. They don't even call them moisturizers or skin fresheners anymore. They call them wrinkle creams and youth enhancers and lip plumpers. Our mothers would sit at their vanity tables and put on plain cold cream at night and simple lanolin in the morning, but we have antiaging serums, special moisturizers with "lift ingredients," line reducers, firming eye creams, and diminishing gels. The mass media that for so long ignored anyone over fifty is desperate to sell us products that will help us "combat" aging. They feel our panic and urge we stall it with spandex and underwire and magical creams.

If we can't have actual youth maybe they can sell us on "youthful." A study showed that one in six Americans becomes depressed when thinking of growing older. That figure came from a Gallup poll that was put out by a cosmetic company, selling (guess what) antiaging cream. One in three women said they will do whatever it takes to stay looking young, that they believe that old is "out" and age defying is "in."

Some stand up to it, like Sissy, a former dancer:

> *I realize I miss being the object of desire because of my beauty. That was my power. On the other hand, I'm so glad that's not ruling my life. I live in L.A. and I'll read about some actress, who I was counting on not to not give in, who has had a face lift. It crosses your mind because everybody seems to do it. The physical changes are hard, but then I see my daughter who at twenty is so upset because she can't fit into skinny clothes. I used to have beautiful sexy arms and now I cover them because I don't think they're beautiful anymore. But when it's 106 degrees outside I think, come on. Maybe in a few more years I won't care. It's possible.*

We're not supposed to like everyday faces. We're supposed to want ones that look like the models'—a way we never looked even when we were that young or that thin. If we looked at real faces more that weren't digitally improved or airbrushed, we'd get used to those little pillowy things that soften the jaw line and happen to every single face. It's like Lulu, a former L.A. woman, says: "The first time I looked in the mirror and saw these lines I thought, 'You are old,' but after a couple of years I got used to them. You adjust."

Hip-Shaking Mamas

It's rather tribal, gathering mornings to let it all out, a valiant group of line dancers in leotards and tights. If you go to the early morning aerobics class you don't have to dress. You can have bed hair. Just brush your teeth and show up. People like to complain about exercise, like it's a punishment or penance imposed from the outside, the results of which will be judged by any number of body watchers with impossible rating sheets. The grown-up approach to exercise is to do it for yourself, the perks coming from how you feel and look to yourself, not to some fickle surveyor of female body parts. As Iris says:

> I would not spend all this time exercising for
> men who aren't going to look at me anyhow. I've
> stopped obsessing on my butt and how it looks.
> Now I'm going for strength and muscle definition.

When you consider how much we depend on our bodies–our personal machines–to get us through the day, it makes perfect sense to give them an hour or so a day of oiling and priming their parts. Think of that when you're in your ratty sweatshirt driving in a cold car to the gym. Think of all the things you're going to ask your body to do that day. To sit at a computer without destroying your neck, wrists, and shoulders; to hold your head nobly; to keep down the stress monger; and walk without a hitch in your hip. To fit into your pants and bend down and pick up assorted babies and small animals without grimacing.

Plus, exercise improves circulation, lowers blood pressure, and helps every tissue get more oxygen, as well as cutting your risk for heart disease and cancer. Why wouldn't you exercise? As long as you can move you can work on the old bod'. And you see all kinds of them at the gym. Real ones of all ages and shapes with their unique bumps and jiggles. The gym and the locker room are great equalizers.

In America the unwritten rule has been that only the tautest bodies can be displayed. They don't have those rules everywhere. Children who grow up going to beaches and parks where their mothers and aunts whip off their tops in the sun seem to have a healthier attitude about women's breasts. Marlene returns to her native Germany enough to appreciate the healthy lack of modesty in her countrywomen:

> *Germans seem to be more comfortable with their bodies and Mother Nature. People don't snicker when they see someone lying in the sun with her top off. They don't say, "She should go on a diet" or "Look at that potbelly." Even their movie stars aren't as perfect as ours. And I think they admire older faces for the character and experience in them, faces that show you have lived, are still here, and can smile.*

At middle age upperarm awareness is very acute, and while you may not be able to hoist your breasts through exercise, you can tone your arms. Not only can you develop arms that make you happy to be sitting under an umbrella table in a sleeveless dress, but there are wondrous things you can do with strong arms. Robin, in her fifties, developed arms she never had at thirty-five or forty-five, just in time to carry around two grandbabies:

> *I decided that one thing I didn't want as I got*
> *older was to get weaker. My partner is a very*
> *active outdoor person and we really enjoy all of*
> *our time together camping, hiking, kayaking. He's*
> *a botanist and I'm a very unscientific bird*
> *watcher. So it's important to me not to get weak.*
> *I do yoga and it's amazing how strong you have*
> *to be for yoga. I still consider myself a yoga*
> *wimp, but I try to walk at least three miles three*
> *or four times a week. And I bought a pair of*
> *eight-pound weights and do curls and lifts in the*
> *mornings.*

Sara began roller blading and kayaking in her late forties: "I don't weigh any less and my stomach is never going to be as flat as it was, but I've restored my joy in using my body."

A strong, healthy woman at any age is a beautiful creature, which is something you finally figure out at the gym. Body strength is appealing, in addition to being quite useful. In her book *Strong Women Stay Young*, Miriam E. Nelson reports that after a year of strength training twice a week, midlife women have been shown to reverse bone loss, develop strength they didn't have when they were young, and enjoy bodies that feel and look ten to fifteen years younger. Tufts University did a study of mostly sedentary women ages fifty to seventy who started doing weight lifting twice a week for forty-five minutes each, and in a year they were 75 percent stronger than before, gaining about three pounds of muscle and losing fat.

The National Institutes of Health calls exercise the most effective antiaging pill, and there are so many varieties of exercise that we can no longer protest that it's boring. Georgie, who dresses like a rodeo queen, was drawn to roller blade aerobics as "the one exercise you can do and wear sequins." Faye, the flight attendant, does yoga:

> *I look in the mirror and think, "Oh god" and then go do two headstands. It's amazing what breath and moving can do for your body. It also helps to turn me around, figuratively and literally, to get a new perspective. If I'm down, I can reverse it and start feeling up. And for the rest of the day I feel a lot lighter.*

Jeanne does Tai Chi, which helps with her arthritis and more:

> *Tai Chi is sufficiently complicated that you can't do it and also think about what's on your desk or what you haven't done. I'm not sure how much shows on me. I think I stand differently. I'm aware of what's going on around me. I'm more aware of my body. I'm stronger. I think my circulation is better. I can leave work at 6 P.M. and tell myself what I really want is a glass of wine and a cat in my lap. But I go to Tai Chi and an hour and a half later I am up and I am back.*

Exercise is also a great way to get through a hot flash, seeing as how you're already red-faced and your hair is hanging in strings. At the gym we get to dance, throwing our bodies around, even if it's just the same old grapevine step, kick, pivot, and turn and singing along to "Love Train."

Kate says women can dance forever:

> *Most men have about ten good dances in them*
> *and then the rest of their life they say they can't*
> *dance until they're drunk. And by then they're off*
> *the beat. So we who are dance deprived can*
> *always find someone to dance with, or at least*
> *next to, at the gym.*

Moving is also good for the brain. Fitness author Jan Todd told *Health* magazine that there's research that shows that running, other vigorous exercise, and mental exercise promote the growth of new neurons while also prolonging the life of existing brain cells. We are creating new learning and memory neurons in the brain–and creating shapely strong arms and cutting our heart risk at the same time.

There's another benefit to getting out of a warm bed and going to a cold gym. A study of women who do weight training showed a correlation between strong bodies and confidence in general. Physical frailty is a liability that translates to psychological timidity, but when women feel good about their bodies—in terms of ability—they are less hesitant and more can-do in other parts of lives. Even Elizabeth Cady Stanton and other suffragists spoke of this, urging women to flex their muscles, so to speak, because physically strong women were less likely to be treated as childlike and dependent.

Physically strong doesn't necessarily mean being skinny. Diana is currently enjoying a weight gain:

> *I like taking up space and I like lying in bed and*
> *feeling my stomach. Another friend who gained*
> *weight said she likes that people have to get out*
> *of her way. If I wanted to be in a relationship*
> *I'd probably try to lose a little of it, and I*
> *wouldn't want to have it become hard for me to*
> *get up and move around. But I want to let my*

body be what it wants to be. I feel more solid,
have more presence.

Whose Breasts Are
These Anyway?

In our culture the bare breasts we commonly see are the ide-
alized ones, naturally round and erect or perfected by
implants. Movie stars have breast doubles so they can appear
to have the perfect ones. So we all have an unrealistic breast
standard. When writer Carolyn Latteier interviewed women
for her book *Breasts, the Women's Perspective on an American
Obsession,* almost every woman said she was dissatisfied with
her breasts: "Media imagery communicates quite clearly that
the best breast—the breast as it should be—is the adolescent
breast. The nipple is smooth, not the lumpy, bumpy nipple of
women who have nursed a baby or outlived their youth. The
reality is that breasts vary as widely as faces. It is every
woman's secret that hers are different" (6).

The middle-aged woman looks down on her breasts, literally, since no underwire is a match for gravity. "After forty-
five, don't even attempt to take the pencil test," says Sydney.

Sara says that at about the time you get old enough to
start feeling at home with them and stop worrying about their
size, you begin to stress over their health:

> *I know so many women my age with breast*
> *cancer that I've started to think that it's almost a*
> *foregone conclusion that I will get it. I'm paying*
> *very close attention so I can catch it as soon as*
> *possible. Every time I hear of another woman*
> *with breast cancer I automatically start feeling for*
> *lumps.*

Patsy had breast reconstruction after a double mastectomy:

> *I had beautiful tits. A nice set, as they used to say, 36D. After they were gone it was kind of an adventure to not have breasts. I didn't have a great sense of loss, which was surprising. It was like being a kid again when you've got these little nubbins coming. I got implants because I had a lot of pride around my breasts. They're part of my beauty. When I found out I was going to lose them I went into a rage and threw all my makeup and lipsticks on the floor.*
>
> *When I first got my implants I thought they were great, but they're kind of in the way as I get older. Everything else in my body is changing and there they stand, like a couple of soldiers.*

Next Wave

Lulu has a pool table in her living room, black satin sheets on her bed, and an underwater watch with dolphins on it:

> *When I was sixteen I thought that fifty was a grandma in an old dress and an apron who worked in the kitchen and didn't go for walks or do anything physical. I think our kids will have a different idea of fifty because of us. I surf with my seventeen-year-old son's friends, who love to tell him they've gone surfing with his mom.*

Lulu got into serious surfing at age 49, after giving it up for almost 30 years.

Then one day I was working in the restaurant and one of the waitresses came back from surfing and said the dolphins were out. I thought, "I'm too old and the water is too cold," but I grabbed my boss's board and went. Surfing is a cosmic experience. The dolphins come around to play. I've been out there when there are seven at a time, four at the end of my board leaping in front of me. People say they can tell when I've been surfing because I'm so happy and calm.

Now I've moved to Hawaii because the surf is better. I think of surfing as something a person can do forever. Of course I've slowed down. You can get hurt. When I was fifty-two the board flipped on me and smacked into my chest. It actually bruised my heart. I couldn't surf for six weeks.

My father was always an exercise nut and I feel I need to do something physical every day to feel good. If I can't do it one way, I find another. Before surfing it was running, ice hockey, and boxing. I think being physically strong makes me determined to not limit myself in other ways. The really big mental thing I've been working on lately is my fear of big waves, which I'm determined to get over. I work hard to feel comfortable in different situations, whether it's choppy surf, going to a party alone, or talking in front of people.

It's Still about Choice

As the twenty-first century began plastic surgeons were performing some 700,000 procedures a year, 70 percent more

than the early part of the 1990s. Baby boomers, who make up
40 percent of the market, went mostly for eye lifts and lipo-
suction. For women and men over fifty, eyelid surgery, to
correct droopy eyelids and bags, was the most common cosmetic surgery. But you could also have your neck skin
cinched and your forehead frozen in a way that you would
never make frown lines again. Even the "redundant skin" (as
some put it) that hangs from your upper arm could be cut
and pasted. For the generation that grew up with more
choices than women before them, here was even more to
decide on.

Erica lives in South Florida surrounded by billboards
and TV ads for cosmetic surgery. Yet, it still surprises her she
went that route:

> *I'm not into messing with my hair or makeup,*
> *and I've never been a real primper. But I like to*
> *look good. I want to look as good as I can for*
> *my age.*
>
> *When I was forty-nine I went for a breast*
> *reduction. I play lots of tennis and had a lot of*
> *back and shoulder pain, which my physical*
> *therapist said could be helped by decreasing my*
> *breast size. I didn't do it right away. I remember*
> *feeling a little bit guilty because about the same*
> *time a friend of mine got breast cancer and my*
> *wants seemed vain and silly compared to someone*
> *with a real problem. My family convinced me to*
> *do it because of my back pain. Then when I saw*
> *the surgeon I decided to ask him what I could do*
> *about the loose skin around my stomach. So I*
> *ended up getting a tummy tuck, too. I was a*
> *little surprised at the huge scar that now runs*
> *from one hip to the other, even though I'm happy*
> *I did it. The best part, though, is that I went*

from a 36D to a 36C and there's no more back pain. Plus I don't have to wear industrial strength bras anymore. I can even go braless.

A year after that surgery I decided to get my eyelids lifted and while I was there, I asked about tightening the skin on my neck and chin. My doctor and I were going for the best that I could look at fifty-one, not to look like a different person. I think I look much better, but it's nothing you could put your finger on—no loose skin around the jaw, a more defined chin and jawline, and eyes that don't look so tired and are open. I'm not sure how my choice will affect my daughters. One had an eating disorder when she was younger and is very conscious of her looks. The other is very comfortable with hers. We live in a body-conscious part of the country. My daughters know a lot of women who've had cosmetic surgery, including their friends and their friends' mothers. Mostly breast implants and noses.

At the other end of the country Rose, a Seattle consultant, says she feels like she pulled off "the coup of the century." When she moved to the northwest at age forty-three she discovered that most people whom she met and associated with were four to twelve years younger than she:

I was meeting people through my three-year-old, and since I had him at the upper age limit, this was inevitable. By the time I reached fifty I was starting to get lines and I just hated looking in the mirror. I was pretty active—tennis, yoga, hiking—so I felt forty and looked fifty.

I consulted with a doctor recommended by a friend. He explained that what I didn't like about my face was basically that the fat had slipped in my cheeks. I liked the idea of moving fat back up the cheekbones. I also decided to have my forehead pulled up and laser surgery around my eyes for a few wrinkles. He said it wouldn't drastically change my looks, but I would look like I had been on a relaxing vacation. That is basically what happened. Now I look more forty-one than fifty-one.

Keeping it a secret was important. If people knew I would feel it defeated the purpose, which was to look ten years younger. I want people to look at me and think I am early forties and looking good. I planned the surgery during the summer, told friends I was going out of town for two weeks, and sent my children to two weeks of summer camp. The only ones who knew were my mother, who helped finance the procedure and take care of me, and my husband. I think my mother thought it was scary, but now she says she's tempted to do her eyelids.

I had two months before I went public. And no one noticed. I think I looked like I used to look and people simply forgot that I was getting saggy cheeks and little lines under my eyes.

Georgie was all set to do the same. She sold her car to get the money, booked her vacation time to recuperate from surgery, and scheduled two friends to bring her food and books and keep her secret. But two days before her facelift, Georgie had second thoughts:

My surgeon wanted me to have an EKG before he operated, and the EKG showed I had some sort of irregular heartbeat and possible valve problem. Both he and my regular doctor said I could still go ahead, that an irregular heartbeat is not that uncommon. But I looked at it as the perfect out. The EKG was telling me I could risk dying just for a new face. After I cancelled I saw an old friend who had a facelift and she looked strange to me, not like I remembered her. So that reinforced my decision because I don't want to look like someone else. Now I'm trying to remember why I thought I needed it. I used to go to this doctor for collagen shots to ease the fine lines and the last time he put the brightest light in the world on my neck, pulled at the skin, and said, "You need more than collagen to repair that." Then I was at a wedding and this guy told me if I ever wanted another date I better have a facelift. I think he was being spiteful because I had once turned him down. Anyhow, I try not to worry about my looks as much anymore. I spent my facelift money on a trip to Turkey and Greece.

Right to Dye

Writer Carolyn Heilbrun, who wears her gray hair in a bun, told interviewer Kate Mulligan that she understands that other women may feel the need to make alterations. "You're going into a forest where no one's been and there are dangers. So if you need camouflage, dye your hair."

Sam has a corporate job in Boston and keeps her long hair brown:

When I hit fifty I really gave some thought to how I'm supposed to dress now and what is my

*hair supposed to look like. I tried being blonde
for a while and then I worried that I would look
like I was trying to pass myself off as someone
younger, like that old expression of mutton
dressed as lamb. You don't want to have this
long blonde hair and then turn around with
wrinkles.*

Marylu, whose short hair is ashen blonde in the front
and brown in the back, asked her hairdresser for something
different:

*I wanted it to look really phony, obviously done.
Arty. Rebellious. But not like the streaks my kids
do.*

Teresa pats her golden curls and explains that she dyed
her hair to embolden herself, after experiencing ten years of
deaths—her son's from AIDS and her parents' from Alzheimer's disease and cancer:

*Four years of AIDS with my son left me gray. My
hair turned gray. My face turned gray. I wanted
color. Life.*

Teresa also keeps a wig for when she and her Texas sisters get together, take over the nearest karaoke bar, and do
their sister song and dance act.

Patricia, on her way to Pakistan to work as a nurse in a
refugee camp, is contemplating letting her long, dyed-black
hair go all-the-way gray while far from home since she'll have
to keep it covered anyway in respect to the prevailing Muslim
tradition:

*When it first started to come in gray I thought it
would be salt and pepper, but it came in dull. So
I dyed it. That startled my children because I've*

*done everything else so naturally. Maybe I'll let it
go while I'm gone, but I want it to come in
white and regal.*

Sara has been streaking her long, brown hair with bands
of gold since she started to go gray in her thirties but she's
tempted to let it come in white as she nears fifty. But she
wouldn't stop there. After seeing a woman at a concert whose
silver hair was enhanced by turquoise and purple streaks, Sara
is inspired to experiment with flashes of color:

*I love that a woman can have a fabulous,
outrageous hairstyle and it simply suits her, rather
than looking like young hair plopped on an aging
person. I guess hair is kind of like jewelry and
clothes, and we're constantly striving to find what
suits and flatters us. What we come up with may
not be what was given biologically at any stage
of our lives.*

Aileen's hair was platinum blonde as a little girl, and she
has a silver mane today. She never considered dying it, even
when her daughter once asked her to:

*When the first gray hairs sprang out my daughter
was still very young and she said, "I don't want
a gray mommy" and I told her, "Sorry, but that
looks like what you're going to get." It became
really gray in my forties, and everyone liked it so
much I saw no reason to change it. Men actually
say they love my hair and women look at me in
the restroom and tell me I'm so brave to go gray.
To me it's an act of defiance. It's about not
being a doll for some man. My father
disapproves. His wives all dyed their hair.*

When Roberta's hair started to turn gray she thought it made her look more professional for her counseling job:

> *I always had a young face and a touch of gray hair gave me credibility. Now I dye it. For a while it served me, then I started to get lines in my face and the hair was too much. Maybe when I'm sixty I'll let my gray hair happen.*

3

Up with Menopause

I still get that twinge that I'm ovulating. I imagine that there's one egg in there and it's using a walker and asking, "Did everyone else get on the bus?"

—Jeanne

My doctor told me, "Think of it like this. Your uterus is dying."

—Penelope

I'm not sure if we can blame all our frustrations on hormones. It's hard to distinguish between what is menopausal and what is just this time on earth.

—Barbara

Burn, Baby, Burn

The average hot flash lasts three minutes, which some literature downplays as "only" three minutes. Three minutes of many things sustained can feel like a lifetime: Three minutes in an attic with a bat. Three minutes stuck in an elevator.

Some women are said to have twenty hot flashes in a day. That could be one hour of being on fire and having your heart beat so fast you think it might fly out of your chest. Still, no one ever died from one. A flash is like a labor contraction, in that if you understand where it comes from and that it will end and not do serious damage, you can approach it as a participant instead of a hapless victim. However, unlike a labor contraction, there is nothing major to show for it when it's over, except maybe a wet blouse and a healthy blush.

While some women's accounts sound like the fever stages of some tropical disease, the average hot flash is mostly uncomfortable and annoying. It gets in the way but it passes. Helen has mixed feelings:

I feel like a hot flash is a kind of purification. Those are my good days. Other times I feel embarrassed to be suddenly sweating.

Rachel sees a double standard:

Athletes don't mind people seeing them sweat and get red-faced. But a woman turning red and fanning herself might be telling the world she's menopausal. And that means she's getting old, and we don't want people to identify us as old. If hot flashes were identified with ovulating they'd be a sexy thing.

The hot flash, however, does belong to menopause. Robin looks at the bigger meaning:

> *It's a sign in a Darwinian sense that we're now useless—no more reproducing—and that a host of medical problems may soon occur. We are put on notice that we're entering a new stage, and all passages are intimidating. On the down side, we're closer to the end than before, but on the plus side, it's very liberating.*

"Try riding your hot flash like a wave," said a leader of a workshop on meditation and menopause. "Don't fight it. Experience it." Cindy's a hypnotherapist whose hot flash maintenance includes martial arts, no caffeine, one hour of meditation a day, and natural progesterone cream instead of hormone pills. She thinks it's possible to actually gain insight and illumination during these electrifying moments. Cindy advises sharing one with your partner, particularly if he's male and knows nothing about hot flashes: "Have him hold your hand and feel your energy. Let him in on the mystery."

To monitor a hot flash in the privacy of your home is one thing, but there is no scheduling them. You could be standing in front of a class or arguing with an editor and suddenly you're a boiled shrimp. We'll know we've put menopause in perspective when we can flash and say "Pardon me" as if we were hit with the hiccups. Most women will not stand up and announce they're flashing, but there are code phrases. Jane says:

> *I usually get a knowing grin from other women when I say, "Who turned the heat up?" I heard of a wedding where the bridesmaids, in deference to the bride's age, walked down the aisle with battery-operated fans instead of bouquets.*

Some women are brazen. Gretchen had a great-aunt who lived on a farm who would suddenly step back from the stove, dash from the kitchen, yell "Hot flash," and jump into the pond.

Kate says before she had her own she went around borrowing hot flashes from her friends:

> *My old college friend Karen started early with hot flashes, around age forty-five. She'd just moved to San Francisco after more than two decades in suburbia and had just divorced her husband of the same period. Being flustered was a current condition, but this day she was sweat-free, and we were relaxing in a very hip South of Market coffeehouse. She had just commented on our sexy waiter. Maybe it was him or the caffeine, but suddenly Karen announced, "I'm having one." I leaned across the table and felt her forehead like an anxious mother. It was cool, but when she lifted her hands from the black Formica table there were two wet prints, like finger paintings. "That's a hot flash," she said.*

Every woman flashes in her own way. Some sweat buckets. Some get only dewy. Nightsweats, the overpowering warmth that hits you in your sleep, is like waking up with two comforters and a large collie on top of you.

In *Dr. Susan Love's Hormone Book*, she claims that hot flashes are misnamed, that they're really our bodies trying to cool us down. A drop in estrogen levels causes the body's temperature control mechanism to go temporarily out of whack. The blood vessels just under the skin dilate, bringing more blood to the skin and causing flushing. The body then goes into its natural cooling response by sweating.

Taking estrogen often reduces the ferocity of flashes, but even modified they can continue for years. And you can't stop them once they start, any more than you can stop your face from turning red in the middle of a speech.

Most women say their flashing starts around their middle and goes lightly up the torso, into the neck and often into the scalp. "I like to visualize that they are zinging my hair follicles and I will end up with lush, long, curly hair. Or that they're a jump start to my brain which will push forward some brilliant, dormant epiphany," says Kate. Mary encourages us to make the most of our hot flashes: "If we can't run away from a hot flash or stop it, why not go with it? It could be like watching yourself on acid."

Kate's daughter asked her to explain a hot flash:

> *I say it's like a full-body blush, with my body one giant pore, and when it's over my ears are still red. Like sitting in the sauna with my clothes on. A bit overrated.*

The Raging Hormone Debate

Jeanne describes her menopausal state: "I still get that twinge that I'm ovulating. I imagine that there's one egg in there and it's using a walker and asking, "Did everyone else get on the bus?"

At fifty-four, her periods are erratic and she's actually looking forward to hot flashes "because I'm a person who is always cold and I really could use something to warm me up." Jeanne intends to proceed through menopause without hormonal assists, "cold turkey." That she's explaining all this in public and saying the word "menopause" aloud instead of using some sly euphemism like "the change" is illustrative of how far menopause has come as part of social discourse.

"Twelve years ago when I first mentioned menopause, it felt shameful," says Sedonia, after leading a menopause circle for thirty women who ended the day walking through a tunnel of red silk to say good-bye to their periods. "We've stopped being shy about it."

At the beginning of the twenty-first century forty million American women were going through menopause and another twenty million are due to join them in the first decade of the new century. We all may vary in how we handle menopause, but it is another great equalizer. Madonna will go into menopause. So will your ex's young girlfriend.

Something that women once suffered in silence, menopause now fills entire shelves in bookstores. There are menopause products, like personal fans and nightgowns made of moisture-wicking fabric, the kind you wear cross-country skiing so you can sweat and not freeze. Some women hang "Estrogen-Free Zone" signs in office cubbies, and menopause is discussed as much as PMS on sitcoms. For all the talk, you'd think we'd have settled on a few things about menopause, but the debate over what to do about it goes on.

Annuscha is a health educator, and when she went into menopause she worked with an endocrinologist to go the "natural" route, based on a natural progesterone cream and a number of vitamins. Her partner, Goldy, who thought she might get the same advice from her "old hippie doctor," was instead advised to try traditional hormone therapy:

> *I had been on such an emotional roller coaster.*
> *Over the top, snapping at people. The hormones*
> *worked. I started smiling at people. My skin*
> *looked better. I had my sex drive back.*

Annuscha decided she wanted what Goldy had, and so both are now on hormones. But they're skeptical. A study came out linking estrogen to high breast cancer risk, and Annuscha said, "It scared the daylights out of me." She called her doctor, who said she wasn't convinced by the study. Annuscha says she'll stay on hormone pills, but she's wary: "I'm always looking for alternatives."

Goldy is suspect of anything as highly hyped as hormone replacement therapy:

> *I was in advertising and I know how easily*
> *people get sold on a sack of shit. You have to be*
> *your own hunter and find out what's best for*
> *your body. But you don't know what or who to*
> *believe. I don't think the scientific knowledge is*
> *out there. You don't know what adverse effects*
> *it's going to have on you, and at the same time,*
> *if it's making your life better you want it. It's a*
> *shot in the dark.*

Some menopause literature makes a big point of saying that some cultures make less of the event than American women do. Japanese women, you may read, rarely speak of menopause and don't even have a word for hot flash. Gwen is married to a Japanese man, and they have lived in Japan for twenty years. She says that's a myth:

> *The word for hot flash is "nobose" and it is very*
> *much one of the symptoms associated with*
> *"menopausal illness." My Japanese friends confirm*
> *that they suffer hot flashes, some more than*
> *others, just like women everywhere, but for a*
> *long time it wasn't considered proper to complain*
> *about it or discuss it with anyone. Japanese*
> *women were expected to shut up and bear it, just*
> *like American women have been traditionally.*

The main event of menopause is that you stop having periods, which should be reason to cheer and wear white pants confidently for the first time since you were fifteen. But it's the side effects of getting low on estrogen that are the most bothersome—dry skin and hair, hot flashes, a decrease in vaginal lubrication. Plus mood swings, anxiety, irritability like you've had too much coffee, sleeplessness, headaches, heart palpitations, dry eyes, dizziness, and more. But most of those can be modified, and none of it has to be dealt with alone.

Nancy, a nurse, says:

We are a lucky generation to have menopause so openly and respectfully discussed, considering that doctors used to consider it everything from a chronic disease to a mental disorder to nothing but imaginings in a woman's head. Of course, that didn't keep them from throwing a bunch of hormone pills at women and ripping out their uteruses and ovaries. And then pitying them for being used up and no longer able to have babies. Is it any wonder a woman back then would want to hide the fact that menopause was happening to her?

Even though we're not hiding anymore, we still go through it, usually by age fifty-one, and not always easily. Most women around age forty-seven begin the process when the body starts lowering its estrogen production and kicking off a number of symptoms that eventually end in menopause. About 70 percent of women have at least one symptom, along with the cessation of monthly periods. After a year without periods a woman can consider herself officially menopausal.

But the whole stretch, called perimenopause, which includes the years before and during menopause, can take eight to ten years. Some women find menopause a loathsome annoyance. Some cruise through it. Many women, like Diana, feel bad about the end of menstruation: "My blood has been like an old friend. It was sad, at first, to give it up."

Just as we started puberty differently, some with a few pimples on our faces, others growing breasts seemingly overnight, menopausal symptoms are individual. They can knock you on your ear—Sydney knows a woman who took a year's sabbatical to deal with her menopause—or be nothing more than an off day or two.

We're still not of a single mind on how we deal with menopause medically, if at all, and that may never happen. Health studies on the pros and cons of hormone therapy often conflict with each other, and we're still trying to determine if there is any menopause drug that does not deliver as many problems as it purports to take away. The doctors change their minds and so do we. You may start out determined to go through this with no more sustenance than a cup of herbal tea and end up so incapacitated by nightsweats that you're begging for hormone pills. Some women make their decision purely on a medical basis, some on a political one. You hear women say all the time that they'll let nature take its course, but if they start growing hair on their chin, some may decide to rethink their choices.

Feeling Like a Guinea Pig?

The pros and cons of hormone replacement therapy keep it a big raging debate. Hormones (estrogen usually combined with progesterone, which also declines during menopause) can ease some menopause symptoms, and they may also protect the body from developing serious medical problems in the future. On the other hand, they may also encourage more medical problems. One-quarter of American women between the ages of forty-five and sixty-four were taking hormones at the beginning of the century, yet no science has determined whether they're good for us or not. "Is it any wonder we feel like guinea pigs?" says Goldy.

This leaves it to us to decide, based on many factors— family medical history, our doctor's advice, what our sister and mother did, what our best friend thinks, what the neighbor just read in her health magazine and whether we are of a traditional or alternative medical persuasion. According to a Harvard university research study reported in the *Chicago Tribune*, women make decisions on menopause based on four strong factors: their doctor's opinion, media reports, their friends' experiences, and their fear of breast cancer.

Jan started doing her homework in her early forties:

My doctor gave me about three inches of literature on hormone therapy and told me if I was going to make the decision, I should make it intelligently. He didn't advise; I came up with the answer. I was working long hours, sleeping little at night, hot flashes prevailed, and I was cranky. I had no cervical, uterine, or breast cancer in my family. But my father died of a heart attack and I have two aunts with osteoporosis. I could see myself going through menopause in high bitch. I went on hormones.

In terms of the popular estrogen Premarin, which is made from the urine of pregnant mares, there's even an animal rights issue. Marylu decided against estrogen because she has breast cancer in her family. She uses progesterone cream based on a compound of wild yams and rationalizes, "I'd rather smear myself with yam juice than take horse pee any day."

Your menopause choice depends partly on what you fear. Linda says every woman she knows with breast cancer was at one time on hormone replacement therapy, so she's staying away from it:

> *But being small boned I'm at risk for*
> *osteoporosis, and estrogen is considered good for*
> *bones. So I eat a lot of foods made from*
> *soy—tofu, tempeh—because soybeans contain*
> *special compounds that are a natural plant form*
> *of estrogen.*

Basically, the medical books say you want to avoid estrogen if you are at high risk for breast cancer. But if you worry about heart disease, you do want it. This frustrates Margy, an early childhood educator:

> *Is there no way to go through our lives without*
> *fear of something getting you for doing absolutely*
> *nothing but living your life to the fullest? I*
> *started taking hormones for hot flashes and then I*
> *read that estrogen can make me more at risk for*
> *ovarian cancer. I feel like I'm being punished for*
> *trying to relieve my symptoms and be a happier*
> *person. I guess the answer is that we were never*
> *supposed to live beyond forty-five.*

But we are getting heard because middle-aged women are savvy medical consumers. We approach our doctors with lists of questions. We educate ourselves. The National Women's Health Network lists at least twenty different menopause information groups.

Teresa, an attorney, said her doctor urged her to take hormones, but Teresa argued, "Why fix something that isn't broken?" Same with Iris:

I simply did not want to take anything that I could not see was necessary. I had symptoms for about five years and passed through without going on hormones. Being in a lesbian relationship meant I had an empathetic companion through menopause, kind of a built-in support system. That definitely helped me through the low points.

Sydney wanted hormones to even out her mood swings:

I call them my don't-kill-a-man pills. When I started having hot flashes I was also getting a divorce, changing jobs, selling a house, and dealing with my son's adolescence. My mother said, "They'll have you purring like a kitten," which almost made me not take them because I don't like listening to my mother. But yeah, they worked.

Some women find they're okay on estrogen but the addition of progesterone makes them feel "a little bit nuts," as Mary says. "I'd have this very even time when every day was the same, and then I'd become a lunatic."

You would think you could count on your doctor to help out, but that's not always the case. Mary's doctor worked with her to get the dosage comfortable, but you still hear stories of old-style docs. Penelope recalls, "My doctor told me, 'Think of it like this. Your uterus is dying.'" When Kathleen starting having erratic periods, she asked her doctor's advice:

He said "Don't worry, I can make you bleed," like he would slip into his God outfit and make me a woman again. I left him and found a woman osteopath, and she put me on very low-level hormones, mostly because I have heart

*disease in my family and estrogen is supposed to
be good for your heart. I am not shy about
managing my own health care or about my body.
In the seventies I was in a health film, showing
women how to use a speculum.*

Is This Happening to You?

"The difference between us and our mothers' generation is
that we tell everything," says Shirley, an herbalist who this
night is scheduled to lead a talk on vaginal dryness with her
menopause group. "We're big mouths. When I ask women of
my mother's time how menopause was, they say it was nothing, or that it was awful but they can't remember anything
else."

That's not a problem with this group, which meets
twice a month to talk about menopause and anything, hormonal and otherwise, in their way at the moment. In the sixties
and seventies this would have been called a consciousness-
raising group, but the contemporary style is less structured
and the food is better than what you might remember. This
night it's Portuguese soup ("goddess food," says Diane) and
Sauvignon Blanc, thanks to the winemaker in the group. The
group came together when two friends, a Head Start teacher
and an educator in a public health clinic, began swapping talk
about menopause, suspecting they were both on the brink and
feeling unprepared. They decided to each grab a couple of
friends and start a menopause group for the purpose of sharing the good, the bad, and the utterly baffling.

In a few months they became as close as friends can be,
evidenced by the fact that this night they start off talking
about Abby's recent procedure. Abby is the one sitting on the
couch on a pillow and being waited on by her partner, Diane,

because Abby had bladder surgery. She explains what her "bladder sling" looks like and how it works. Part of her tale makes the others want to sit very still and part of it makes them burst out laughing. Everyone in Abby's living room understands why such a procedure might become necessary, having experienced a weak bladder moment during a hearty laugh or sneeze. "It's a reminder," says Shirley, "to do your kegels, those silent, invisible contractions that exercise the vaginal muscles."

Abby says it feels like she just had a baby and explains that having produced "two big hulking kids" had a lot to do with the pressure on her bladder.

Before they get to the night's agenda they detour to mood swings, another subject that brings as many laughs as groans. Barbara says she remembers as a little girl hearing her grandmother and friends talk about what must have been menopause:

> *Someone said, "Miss Emma's going crazy. She's going through the change." Then the women would make her tea and tell her to get some special salve. They'd come around so she'd never have a chance to be depressed. And they'd tell her man, "She's having a time, so be nice to her." As a kid I thought, "Ooh, what does that mean?" Now I'm real clear about how it was for Miss Emma to lose her mind for a while.*

They sound like a twelve-step group reporting in; "It's been sixty days since my last period," says one. Barbara says it's been almost a year and she wishes she would stop once and for all, because she's feeling frantic all the time:

> *That's what's pissing me off. I have to get this over with because I have work to do. I start to think I'm over my periods and then the damn*

*thing comes. Then I'll have three and a half
weeks of PMS and I start praying for a period.*

Shirley, the herbalist, reminds Barbara to take her skull-cap, an herb she says "takes the edge off" and one she calls "the menopausal woman's best friend." She says, "It's for those moments when you want to come out of your skin. When the noise is a little much." Barbara said she tried it one day when her grandson was visiting and she was trying to do some writing:

*It calmed me down, I guess, but I'm not sure if
we can can blame all our frustrations on
hormones. It's hard to distinguish between what is
menopausal and what is just this time on earth.*

When a visitor comments on the candor of the group, noting a side discussion on whether chin hair should be plucked or waxed, Abby says, "It's just life. Why can't we talk about all of it?" Abby was raised by a stepmother who she now realizes suffered alone during menopause:

*She was wacko for a long period and it was the
same time I was going through adolescence, so I
was the devil. She certainly didn't have a group
like this. She had no support at all. She isolated
herself and she seemed to hate everyone. I feel
bad now that I wasn't more understanding. But
before this group, that's all I knew about
menopause.*

All the women here have decided to avoid hormone therapy and go through menopause naturally, although Shirley warns, "That can change, depending on the intensity of your symptoms." She personally relies on herbs to calm hot flashes and mood swings and eats a lot of soy-based foods, which contain natural estrogen. Her nighttime snack is a glass of sherry and a bowl of roasted soy nuts. But Shirley's sister had such debilitating nightsweats she went on estrogen and progesterone pills just to get some sleep.

Shirley brings up the subject of women fading into the scenery as they get older, although it's hard to imagine any of these women not being seen or heard:

> *It's as if we disappeared as sexual beings. I was trying to explain that to my husband, that men don't notice middle-aged women, that they look through us, and he said "That's nonsense," but then he watched at a party and saw what I meant.*

Barbara says it's different in African-American culture:

> *There's a whole different view of being older, just like there is of being big. Men will always give you play no matter your size or age. And black women are good at giving it back to their men. If they say something about us looking older, like "Look at those new gray hairs," we just say, "Well, look at those on you."*

Abby is Mexican-American and says:

> *In Mexican soap operas the romantic characters are older than in American soap operas. I think Mexican men look at young women as what they want when they're having babies, but they also admire the maturity of older women. They look at us as senoras, with wisdom. But here in this country we're told we all have to look like Barbie dolls. We don't allow getting old in this society.*

Abby's the self-appointed vanity queen. She admits that she worries most about her looks changing than any of the others: "I don't want to be twenty or thirty again. I want to know all that I know now, but I don't want my body and face to go." She had a scare when her thick black hair started thinning and was relieved to discover it was a temporary result of the anesthesia from her surgery and not menopausal: "I was crying to Diane, 'Oh no, do we have to go bald, too?'"

One night the group did a ritual where they decorated wooden clothespins with scraps of cloth and paint and named them for their concerns—fear of abandonment, despair, judgment by others—and burned them one by one in the fireplace.

On to vaginal dryness. It's a common complaint that when you get older, vaginal lubrication takes longer and may not be sufficient. Shirley, the researcher in the group, explains:

> *Reduced estrogen and progesterone are directly related to dry skin all over the body, including the vaginal tissues. The vagina and surrounding tissue can lose elasticity and the vagina can become smaller and thinner. But it's the old "use it or lose it" remedy. Regular intercourse stretches the vagina and increases lubrication and blood flow. Masturbation, as well, helps decrease dryness and irritation.*

The group seems pleased with their assignments and wants to talk about lubricants. Abby, the nurse, passes out samples of various products. "AstroGlide? It sounds like something you put in your car," says Leslie. "So male."

"No, sweetie, you put it in you," says Abby. "But if you use too much you'll slip and slide in the wrong places."

Barbara wants to know about estrogen cream. No one has tried it, but Shirley is a believer in using the herb motherwort along with vitamin E to make things juicy.

They end up talking about sex and Barbara says:

I think sex lasts as long as you're not dead. But as I get older I want more from making love. I need more than antics in bed. I call it a mental fuck, another sense of depth. Intimacy. Honoring me. And foreplay. Lots and lots of foreplay.

A chorus of very busy women shout out, "Who has time for foreplay?"

Who Are You Calling Emotional?

Cindy walked into a gift shop in Maui and remarked how the incense and candles reminded her of her menopause and meditation group back home. The shop owner rushed over, pulled her aside, and said, "Tell me all you know about menopause." It turned out the store owner had left the Midwest to move to Hawaii because she suspected she was close to a breakdown or had a brain tumor and wanted to be close to family when she finally succumbed. Once in Hawaii she talked to a doctor who told her she was just going into menopause and wasn't going to die.

Goldy says that when she first noticed menopausal symptoms she was helping to remodel a house, which was causing some stress but not enough to account for her sudden behavior:

I almost killed one of the guys working with us. I was overreacting on everything. Snapping. And I kind of knew it because I would sometimes think, "This isn't really you."

It hit Annuscha at forty-nine:

*I've always been a very optimistic person. I
inherited my mom's happy genes. But then I
started feeling like I wanted to cry and cry."*

Health experts don't agree on whether there is a direct
link between mood swings and the sudden drop in estrogen
and progesterone levels during menopause. However, any
woman who has the mean blues during menopause recognizes
them as an advanced version of PMS.

We can treat them the same way we did PMS. Herbs,
drugs, yoga, a walk in the woods, talking to a friend, dancing
savagely around your living room, or like Adina, indulging
your big, bad mood:

*I feel like I did when I was a teenager in terms
of mood swings. But when I was young, growing
up WASP in England, I suppressed my emotions.
Now, at the other end of the spectrum, I don't
want to suppress them. Sometimes I go into my
car and scream. I was at the bank and a teller
said something that just made me think of crying.
I'm not sure what it was, but I thought, "Here I
go again." The surges of emotion are the same as
at puberty, but now it's thirty-five years later.*

The irritability, anxiety, and depression of menopause
are not unlike the emotions we felt entering adolescence,
after the baby was born, during PMS, and from being on
birth control pills.

Progesterone is thought to have a sedative effect on the
body and estrogen acts like a stimulant. When they work in
tandem, which they normally do before menopause, we feel
balanced. When they're spiking and dipping so are we. Carrie
says, "I either felt like I was having an out-of-body experience
or turning into this raging bitch." Cindy recommends
meditation:

*I was irritable and angry, but instead of reacting
with an outburst, I'd stop, run the scene through
my mind, and think about what outcome I wanted.
I made a choice before I reacted, like stopping a
movie. I didn't want to be a slave to hormone
imbalance and see the look on my children's faces
when I suddenly got mad. I'm going for harmony.*

Jane thought she needed help in therapy:

*I was getting what seemed like PMS, but I'd never
had PMS before. Sudden bad moods for no reason. I
went to my shrink, who said she'd be glad to talk
to me but that I might be better off going to my
gynecologist and talking about getting on hormones.
So I went on estrogen and progesterone, but the
progesterone made me cranky. I tried a different
combination, and now I'm okay.*

For some women hormone replacement therapy may
cause rather than lift their bad moods. Dr. Susan Love
believes hormone pills can actually cause depression. She suggests herbs and homeopathic remedies to deal with mood
swings, and to cope with the fuzzy thinking that a lot of
women also experience she recommends exercising the brain.
Join a book club, take a class, go online.

Mary tried antidepressants:

*When I was forty-eight, I started to feel lousy:
anxious, lethargic, and basically without hope. I
couldn't concentrate and just didn't want to do
anything. My family doctor gave me one type of
pill and then a psychiatrist gave me something
else, which gave me huge hives. Then I got an
antidepressant which made me not care about
anything. I missed deadlines at work. I didn't file*

my taxes until June. I slept all the time. I gained
fifteen pounds. Then I got tired of being tired and
stopped taking them. The weight did not go away
very easily, but I have my memory back and I do
take care of things.

Even if you can't technically connect mood swings to hormones, you can make the link between feeling out of sorts about getting older, facing phobias about aging, and observing body changes that say you are decidedly entering a different time of life. Mary says she started feeling trapped:

I made bad career choices and felt it was too late
to do anything about that. I felt I had nothing to
look forward to in work or in play. By taking the
antidepressants I got to stop feeling bad, which
was necessary. But I wish I'd spent the time
while I was taking the drugs trying to figure out
what made me feel bad and dealing with those
issues instead of, basically, hiding. That's what
seems to be missing from this pill-taking scenario,
the fact that pain comes from something and you
need to find out what causes it instead of just
anesthetizing it. If aging issues were dealt with
more openly, maybe we'd have a clue about what
is making us feel bad.

Georgie tried a number of mood-altering drugs too but finally concluded that she couldn't blame everything on unsettled hormones: "I cried before I was menopausal."

Think of It This Way

The postmenopausal woman, according to Celtic culture, had a definite assigned role to spread her wisdom through the community. Christiane Northrup, author of *Women's Bodies,*

Women's Wisdom, says the young maiden was the flower, the mother was the fruit, and the elder woman was the seed, and that the seed held memory and wisdom. Some cultures, Northrup explains, believe that women at menopause begin to store their blood rather than shedding it, which has them holding on to the wisdom.

Roberta believes that estrogen keeps us more malleable, and that when it lessens we develop more of an edge:

> *Estrogen may be a go-with-the-flow passivity*
> *agent. I used to wonder when I was going to feel*
> *like an adult, with power and authority. When*
> *was I going to stop being afraid. And it's*
> *happening now as I go into menopause. Now that*
> *I have less of that hormone I notice a contrast in*
> *my personality. I'm more willing to speak out.*
> *I'm not as tamped down. We need estrogen so*
> *that we're willing to stay home and be with*
> *those kids and put their needs first. But now I*
> *feel that spunky kid in me is coming out again.*

Kathleen's doctor basically told her the same, and advised she think of menopause as the reverse of puberty: "She said to think about estrogen as what we need when we're being nurturing, but when estrogen leaves you get to be the bold girl again, the one who before her period climbed trees and was fearless."

Dr. Susan Love like this idea too. She says when we lose the "domesticating hormone" of estrogen we can get back some of the blossom and brashness of the young girl.

Skin and Bones

We've all seen the occasional old woman so bent over she's looking at the sidewalk, and we shudder. Or we might glance at the osteoporosis poster of two women in the doctor's office. The one with "normal bones" is smiling and standing straight like she's looking for a dance partner. The other, whose bones in a close-up photo resemble a shell left on the beach, shot full of holes, is bent over a cane. Since health posters are heavy-handed, the woman with good posture is wearing clothes from a fashion magazine and the other is in 1955 Goodwill. But the point is made that we need to pay attention to our bones.

Diane, who swims, kayaks, and rides horses, was stunned when she got a bone density test and found she had early signs of osteoporosis, known as osteopenia. Bone loss actually starts around age thirty-five, when women start losing about half a percent of bone each year. Around menopause there is increased reduction in bone mass, but you don't feel it or see it. Diane's doctor recommended she have her bones measured even though she had no symptoms. She went on hormones, started chugging calcium, and tried to find a new regimen based on a weight-bearing exercise, or something that forces bones to resist gravity:

> *I gave up swimming for walking. But walking is
> such a weather-dependent and time-consuming
> activity. I tried jumping rope and I hated it. I
> tried the weight machines at the gym but never
> really felt like I was getting that much out of it.
> I finally decided I better get serious about it after
> visiting my grandmother, whose mind is fine,
> whose health is otherwise fine, but whose bones
> are not holding her up. Now I go to an exercise
> studio and do intensive weight training with a
> personal trainer twice a week. We are talking
> serious weight-bearing exercise. I love how it
> makes me feel. I'm losing weight without dieting,
> and my bones and joints are getting a thorough*

*but safe workout. It costs a lot, but I figure it's
the best preventive medicine a woman faced with
osteoporosis can offer herself.*

Bones aren't known for their sex appeal. You go to the
gym to work on your abs or your biceps, but who's there for
bones? It's the visible, showy things that usually get the attention. But your bones could be thinning at this very moment
and you wouldn't even know it. It happens out of sight, like
termites in the wall. But it's not one of those things we have
to settle for. It's preventable.

Kate, who has always prided herself on her posture and
eating green vegetables, was also surprised to learn her bones
were thinning:

*Just out of curiosity I asked my doctor about
getting a bone test and she said that since I was
on hormones and there were no apparent risk
factors, my insurance company would never cover
it. But something nagged at me and so the next
time I saw her I said that my sister had a bone
test, implying that it wasn't favorable, and now I
really thought I should get one. Apparently that's
all the reason my doctor needed, because in I
went and the insurance company paid. But I still
was shocked when she called and said "Uh-oh."
How could I fail a bone test?*

Bones don't hurt when they're thinning, but they do many
years later when you fall down and break a hip, which is when
many women discover, too late, that they are osteoporotic. Or
suddenly you'll realize that you are shorter than your daughter
and it's not because she's always wearing high-heeled shoes.
It's because the fragile bones in your spine are crushing.

Bones are attached to muscles, and if you strengthen
your muscles you'll help your bones, so Kate keeps a set of

weights in her office and another by the couch in the living room so that she'll remember to lift them every couple of days. Her doctor increased her estrogen dose and told her that if she was going to keep drinking coffee, which cuts into the calcium in the body, to make sure she added milk to it. She also told her that for calcium pills to work she had to also take vitamin D:

> *I take nine different vitamins but no D.*
> *Apparently you need the D to get the calcium*
> *working right. So all these years I've just been*
> *shooting a calcium bullet through my body that's*
> *not even touching my bones. You can get vitamin*
> *D in a multiple vitamin, but you can't get*
> *enough calcium in a multiple. The best way to*
> *get vitamin D is to sit in the sun, but we know*
> *the risks of that. So, here we go again. Which*
> *part of the body gets served? I chose my bones.*

Vitamin D, which comes from diet and the sun, is so essential to bone building that middle-aged women who live under gray skies lose more bone in the winter than in the summer. Another little known fact about our womanly bones is that skinny people actually break easier when they hit the vulnerable age for osteoporosis. A little added weight, say the experts, can actually provide a nice cushion for when our bones need babying. So even though milk and cheese and chocolate-covered-cherry frozen yogurt might be fattening, our bones will be happier for them. Bone-wise there's a very good reason to celebrate middle-age spread.

One of the arguments for taking hormones at menopause is that estrogen nourishes our skeletons, but not every woman can or wants to go that route.

Adele has stopped taking estrogen:

Who wants to be on a drug without any real reliable studies? Still, I have tiny bones, which means I could get osteoporosis, and I went into menopause young, in my thirties, which also puts me at risk. So I get regular bone scans; eat lots of calcium-rich foods; and run, bicycle, and play tennis.

Aileen can't do hormone supplements because she had breast cancer:

So I lift weights, ski, and hike in the hills. I also do yoga. It's like oiling my body; it keeps me lubricated. I eat tofu, brown rice, and the vitamin K vegetables, like kale and spinach, which are good for bones. I do drink a glass or two of wine a day, which has nothing to do with bones (actually, excessive alcohol use hurts bones), but it's good for my heart. You can always find statistics to support what you want to do for your health, and I've found mine.

What about Those Spots?

We already know what to do for our skin. Wear sunscreen. Drink plenty of water. Don't smoke. Don't drink. Avoid ugly thoughts. Have sex.

Noticeable skin changes start to happen in the mid- to late forties, which is about the time Sara, who never wears makeup except for an occasional lipstick, spent one hundred dollars on a moisturizer that made her sister-in-law's face glisten and glow. Around the age of forty-seven is when perimenopause hits, causing estrogen production to slacken, which is pretty much what happens to skin, too, even though skin changes are generally attributed more to aging than loss of estrogen. There are no scientific studies to show that taking estrogen will smooth out wrinkles, but it might be possible that estrogen causes the facial skin to retain fluids, and the result is that some lines are filled out.

The condition of your middle-aged skin depends on how much time you fried in the sun as a kid, if and how long you smoked, and your family's strong jaw line. There are inevitable changes, usually first spotted on the face. But skin is skin. Maria complains about the "lizard skin" on her legs and Maureen speaks of "leather cleavages" of sun-fried bosoms.

Rachel is used to having freckles, but she frowns at one new dark spot on her hand:

> *This is not a freckle. This is an age spot. It*
> *reminds me of my mother. It looks old. I'm*
> *waiting for my son to look at me one day and*
> *say, "Why are you so old? I want a younger*
> *mother." I asked my husband the other day if he*
> *noticed that my face has these new little lines*
> *and he said, "You've always had those lines."*

At fifty the connective tissues start to lose strength and elasticity. You finally see what it means to make a face and have it freeze like that. Wake up with pillow creases on your cheeks and they may be there past breakfast. This is the age when the brown spots from old sun damage come back to haunt and stay. And suddenly there are new moles and skin tags, tiny flaps of skin. Most skin growths are not dangerous but because there are so many of them seemingly arriving daily, many of us may spend a lot of time asking our doctors if this is skin cancer or just another middle-aged skin thing.

Jane spent most of her adult years covering up at the beach, but she still didn't escape:

We all got sun damage long before SPF was invented. I went to my dermatologist to have a brown spot removed, but when he dug too deep and left a silver spot on my nose I went to a plastic surgeon for laser treatment on the other spots. I had about nine or ten taken off—red spots, brown spots, some moles. They gave me Valium and I went back to work with teeny Band-Aids all over my face.

Kate says her doctor told her that some women come in wanting spots removed that she can't even see:

My doctor asked one woman if she spent all her time with a magnifying glass looking for new spots and she said yes. I think she told me this because I was being obsessive about my own spots and wondering if taking hormone pills causes them. She told me that when we're taking estrogen it's the same as when we were taking birth control pills and when we were pregnant. More hormones cause sun sensitivity, so what we once called the mask of pregnancy is now those little potato skin-colored patches on the face.

There are other skin changes with pet nick-names—crow's-feet, which are the smile lines beside your eyes; bunny lines, the ones by the nose; and, of course, liver spots, the brown dots on your hands. There are ways to minimize all of them now with laser treatments, chemical peels, and collagen. Or we can bravely just ignore them, like Kate is doing with her brown spots:

I've had brown spots on my hands ever since I spent most of one summer out in a canoe. I remember coming back from that trip and a

friend said "Ooh, where did those come from?"
and I told her I guess I'd fried my hands. I was
thirty-five at the time. Through the years different
friends have suggested different creams or bleaches
I could try to eliminate them. One even
whispered that I could borrow her Retin-A. I now
see there's a laser treatment for one thousand
dollars or more that maybe could zap them. I
mentioned it to my daughter and she said,
"You've always had those spots," and certainly in
her life I have. She said they wouldn't be "mom
hands" without them. I can use one thousand
dollars on other things.

My Uterus, Myself

In the time of our foremothers, a hysterectomy, which is the removal of the uterus, was a whispered thing, but it was also pretty standard procedure for women hovering near menopause. The very word was off-putting, linked as it was to hysteria, a mental disorder peculiar to women. They're still pretty common.

After Sukie's doctor told her she needed a hysterectomy she made the rounds of her favorite hair salons, "going to the source" for information:

My doctor could tell me what he was going to
do and why he needed to do it, but I needed to
talk to other women who had gone through the
same thing so I would know what to expect. I
asked all my hairdresser friends who they knew
who'd had a hysterectomy, and pretty soon I had
a list of names and phone numbers along with all
the second-hand advice my hairdresser friends had

picked up from their clients.
I found out that there wasn't much
recuperation time after the surgery and that my
sex life would not be over. One hairdresser said,
"Women tell me you just get dry afterward, but I
think you can buy something for that." The next
hairdresser knew what to buy.

For a long time medical men had women convinced that the uterus was directly tied to the brain, so that if you tinkered with one you'd affect the other. Some used this theory to argue that if women used their heads too much to become educated they'd weaken their ability to carry babies. Of course, they didn't follow this logic to the other side, to conclude that once a woman stopped being fertile she could concentrate on her brains and become very wise.

Renaissance doctors believed that as women got older the womb sometimes became detached from its place and wandered about inside the body, causing uncontrolled behavior. And since the popular remedy for crazy behavior was to find something to remove, a favorite was the uterus. "With a middle-aged woman patient, when the surgeon thinks, 'What should I take out,' the word uterus darts through his mind first," wrote Mary Ellmann in 1968 in her book *Thinking About Women.*

Even though removing the uterus of a middle-aged woman is still common, with the United States leading the world in number of hysterectomies, women don't keep it a secret like they once did. Sara went to a "womb party" at the beach where her friend, who had had a hysterectomy, buried her uterus. But that was in California.

Sandie, a nurse, had her hysterectomy quietly:

One day I started hemorrhaging. I had just
turned fifty and hadn't started menopause. They

*took me to the emergency room. I remember it
was the Celtics play-offs. They said I should have
a hysterectomy and I protested, "Not so close to
golfing season." Five weeks later I was on the
golf course, without my uterus.*

Laura is a teacher, and when she was about forty-two
her periods turned to floods:

*The girl students would furtively whisper that I
had blood on my skirt. I was so humiliated
because this was supposed to be happening to
them, not me. Finally, after years of being
chronically anemic, taking to my bed, and using
towels for pads, I insisted that my gynecologist do
something. He said to hang on, avoid taking
aspirin, and that it would stop in a few years
when I started menopause.*

*I went to another gynecologist, a woman,
who gave me a simple one-hour operation under
epidural anesthesia. At one point she told me that
all the parts were out, and I asked to hold them.
She obliged by passing my uterus and ovaries
across my draped legs. The uterus was about the
size and shape of a very small pear. The ovaries
were like tiny oysters and the fallopian tubes
were tiny noodle-like appendages. Holding my
reproductive organs was a great cathartic
experience. They'd served me well. Now I could
bid them good-bye with pleasure.*

*In four weeks I was riding my bike on the
beach at Hilton Head. And it gave me back the
freedom to leave my house without a grocery
sack full of tampons and pads. Three years later
I'm convinced it was the best thing for me. The*

*surgery took me right into menopause, so I
started taking estrogen supplements right away.
But I never had a hot flash or any problems with
my sex life. It takes longer to get things going,
but my husband and I are doing fine.*

The source of Laura's bleeding was uterine fibroid tumors, which occur in 25 percent of women and are the reason behind one-third of all hysterectomies. Fibroids are benign growths in the muscular tissue of the uterus and are fueled by estrogen. Women approaching menopause often experience increased fibroid growth. If you can hold out, they tend to shrink after menopause. In the meantime they can cause backaches and swollen stomachs, pelvic pain, cramping, bladder pressure, and lots of bleeding. "Sixty pads in a five-day period," said Cynthia, explaining why she went seeking relief.

This popular procedure accounts for one in three American women having her uterus removed by age sixty, compared to one in eighteen in France, according to health writer Natalie Angier. But, like many old standards, it does have its skeptics. Christine, who was all ready to go that route, says, "Some women think hysterectomy is the answer. Some think it's castration."

It once was common practice to take out the ovaries as well as the uterus, kind of a two-for-one offering by your surgeon, the old "as long as we're in there," attitude. This has been challenged by women like Christine, who wondered if the same surgeon might reasonably ask of a man, "As long as we're in there, would you like to have your testicles taken out, sir?" Some women opt for a partial hysterectomy. Take the uterus, leave the ovaries. This way you stop bleeding but don't automatically go into menopause. Carol had her uterus removed at forty-two because of fibroids, but she kept her ovaries and still has no menopause symptoms at age fifty.

The hysterectomy debate has pushed medical science to consider less invasive procedures to remove fibroids, which happened just in time for Christine:

"Hysterectomy" is such a loaded word. Years ago a doctor had encouraged me to have one for fibroids. I told her I wanted to hang onto my uterus. The doctor asked why, and I said, "Because I'm attached to it." Doctors act like it's a useless organ and it has only to do with reproduction. I'm not sure that's true. Besides, I knew that not everyone has an easy time with it and I also worry about the risks of anesthesia. But I carried around a grapefruit-sized fibroid for twelve years, and I finally was so miserable I gave in and scheduled a hysterectomy.

Then my husband read a newspaper story about an alternative procedure called fibroid embolization, which shrinks fibroids by blocking their blood supply. My doctor hadn't suggested it; in fact he told me that if I were his wife he would want me to have at least a partial hysterectomy. I got on the internet, read about it, decided it was a minimally invasive but legitimate procedure, cancelled my surgery, and found someone nearby to do it. With a hysterectomy I'd planned on taking a month off, but after the embolization, which I had done as an outpatient, I was back to my stretch class in three days, and in seven days I was back to work. The most satisfying thing is now I can go to the symphony and not have to run to the bathroom before, during, and after the performance.

Roberta's mother had a hysterectomy for fibroid tumors in her forties, and when Roberta developed them in her forties the first gynecologist she saw advised she do the same:

He examined me for maybe thirty seconds and said I should have a hysterectomy—uterus, ovaries, cervix, take it all out. I said I wanted to keep my ovaries if they were still okay because I wasn't convinced that once they stop making eggs they aren't still doing something valuable. He didn't like that idea. Then when I told him I wanted to keep my cervix because I thought it was important for sexual pleasure he kind of laughed. I never went back to him and told my family doctor to never refer another woman to that guy.

4

Stoke the Fire

I want a man who is willing to work at being intimate.

—Aileen

Just admit that you want to hang out with fourteen-year-olds, but don't say I'm not beautiful.

—Barbara

I started feeling sorry for teenage boys and how they're always horny. I just wanted it all the time. I even started fantasizing about the bus driver.

—Carrie

I'm scared to death because I have so much to lose, and I know that I do much better as a functioning human being when I'm not in love. But given the opportunity, I'll take passion every time.

—Sam

We take our glasses off when we have sex. This way we're both blind when we're naked, so no matter how old we get we'll always look the same to each other, in a blurred way.

—Anne

Red Hot Mamas

At step-aerobics, the teacher was singing along to, "You can ring my bell. . . . Dingalingaling," when she suddenly pivoted and, without missing a beat, deadpanned, "*That's* been a while."

This got her an automatic and sympathetic groan from her class, all women of a certain age. Kate says, "We've become the ones who joke about 'not getting enough' from some of the same boys who twenty-five years ago were grousing the same thing about us."

It would appear that contrary to mythology, middle-aged women like sex more than some of their male peers do. In an anthology on middle age called *Are You Old Enough to Read this Book?*, author John Gray discusses the differences in sexual heat among middle age couples and says it's common for women over fifty to be more in touch with their desire for sex and for their male peers to be less so. Sue hypothesizes that as young women we paced ourselves and they didn't:

> *They used up all their erections early, starting*
> *from birth for godsake, and so by the time*
> *they're fifty it's no wonder they don't come up as*
> *sure as the sun every morning. And we, who*
> *spent all those years being in charge of birth*
> *control, experimenting with various unsatisfactory*
> *methods and praying to Our Lady of Monthly*
> *Reprieves, can finally relax.*

Unless we're out on the circuit and definitely need to practice safe sex, we old married ones can now romp to our heart's delight. "No more waiting for him to snap on a rubber or running to the bathroom for the can of foam," says Kate, "no more debating his getting a vasectomy or you a tubal. We're paraphernalia-free and just waiting on the big guy."

In her sexy book *Spending*, about a middle-aged woman who meets not only a muse for her art but a rollicking good lover, Mary Gordon writes an appreciation of sex over age fifty: "At this historical moment having good sex or even the prospect of it is like having a lot of money and living among people who are barely getting by" (49).

Sukie thinks sex gets better after menopause: "You can enjoy it more. You don't have to worry about getting pregnant, and you've stopped caring if he thinks you're a slut and won't respect you in the morning."

But there is this old myth that good sex is pretty much over at middle age, says Lynn:

> *I called my therapist to ask if women in their forties are always horny. She said, "Yes they are." I was wondering if I was getting ready for menopause and after that I wouldn't be horny ever again. I was starting to panic, like I better hurry up and sample all the chocolates in the box now.*

Not to worry. Dr. Nancy Snyderman assures us in her book *Dr. Nancy Snyderman's Guide to Good Health for Women Over Fifty* that the clitoris does not appear to be affected at all by aging and that in fact many women are more orgasmic after menopause. Same with Natalie Angier, who writes, "The clitoris is always there for you" in her book *Woman: An Intimate Geography*. Plus there's evidence that we've reached the age where sex is the prudent thing. The *Women's Health Advocate* hinted that sex could be right up there with vitamin C in preventing colds, citing a 1999 study at Wilkes University, which showed that people with few or no sexual encounters may be at greater risk for catching a cold than those who have sex regularly.

Jillian, an artist who always had an active sex life, found that there are some stumbling blocks that have to be dealt with at menopause:

> *Suddenly it hurt just to get a Pap test. I tried all the gooey lubricants, but lubrication wasn't the issue. It was what was going on inside. My doctor said my vaginal walls were paper thin. She called it vaginal atrophy. Ouch.*
>
> *I didn't have a boyfriend at the time so I just put off dealing with the problem. She said I could use estrogen cream, which will eventually strengthen the tissues, but you can't use estrogen without some kind of progesterone and the progesterone in hormone pills always made me a little crazy. Finally she came up with a combination estrogen and progesterone cream and I think it might work. Now I'm looking for someone to love, at least long enough to practice on.*

Some women just go dormant for a while. Pamela, an insurance executive, said she was celibate for five years and figured that was it, "But the other day I met a man and started to have those old stirrings, and I thought, 'All right, I'm back.'"

Sue's eighty-year-old friend gave her a bottle of massage oil once when she was going to meet a boyfriend: "She told me to crawl under the covers nude and ask him to rub it all over me. She said it's good for the skin and we need to do it regularly, and I don't think she meant the oil."

In her book *Second Chances*, novelist Alice Adams wrote a romantic story about a middle-aged couple who made love every Sunday morning. She describes this passionate pair so convincingly you hope she knew about it firsthand. They would stay in bed and smoke a joint and have long leisurely reciprocal sex every Sunday. Key word: leisurely.

At a menopause circle several women, including Angie, talked about wanting a different speed and style of sex: "Sex based on tenderness, no grabbing, less acrobatics, more talking. I like that sex takes longer now that we're older, even if that's only because we don't roll as easily as we once did."

According to a 1998 study by the National Council on Aging, more than half of Americans over sixty say they have sex at least once a month. Forty percent said they wished they had more and close to 75 percent said they enjoyed sex as much as—or more than—when they were forty. So, there's something to look forward to—at least once a month. The forward-thinking Finns held a middle-aged lovemaking celebration in the summer of 1999 near Helsinki, with trails pointing couples to secluded meadows. It was to commemorate the International Year of the Older Person and to show that there's no age limit to a good romp. An AARP study in 1999 found that people continue to view their partners as romantic and physically attractive at all ages. But sometimes you have to work at it. Annascha says:

> The joke is, "What do lesbians over forty fantasize about?" The punch line is "Sleep." I think there's decreased libido as you get older and it doesn't matter who you're with. We make a date. We make dinner and get a movie . . . and then fall asleep. And say, "For sure, tomorrow night." Two years ago we turned off our cable service. We sit and talk. We read to each other, and argue about what's in the newspaper. But we don't say, "I'm horny. Why aren't you?"

Her partner, Goldy, elaborates:

*You don't always have to have sex. You can
massage each other. You can see how long you
can kiss. Can you kiss for two hours?*

Of course, some women would still choose to say "No,
thanks." Germaine Greer and even Colette wrote happily
about being postsexual. Francine du Plessix Gray wrote in the
New Yorker, "The more fortunate among us serenely accept
that we may never again be seen as objects of erotic desire . . .
that we must acquire instead a deepened inward gaze."

Pam was celibate for seven years. If you ask her if she
missed sex, she says:

*There's machinery. I decided to take a break from
men for a while and made that choice to be
celibate. I was having indiscriminate relationships
without integrity and not getting that much out
of it. So I just quit. I can turn off the receptors.
I don't want to attract men like I did when I
was younger. But I have felt reawakened lately. I
know what I want this time in a relationship. I
want to relate to someone intellectually. I want
someone who doesn't need to consume me. I
need a lot of alone time.*

For those who still want to stoke the fire, there is an
ever-growing number of vaginal assists that you can buy over
the counter. Astroglide and Aqua Lube sound like something
you find in a hardware store, but there is no doubting who
the cream called Vital Vulva is intended for. The books
encourage visualization to get things flowing. Imagine your
vagina being pink, wet, pulsating. A hot lava image works. Jillian says she can get warm thinking about a guy on a motorcycle with a black T-shirt.

Carrie had bus driver fantasies, but that had to do with an overdose of testosterone:

After I had a hysterectomy my doctor put me on estrogen, but that set off my migraines so I stopped taking estrogen, and then I started crying all the time. I wanted to run away. I didn't like my husband, kids, no one. I couldn't stand it, so I called the first woman doctor I saw in the Yellow Pages *and that's how I met a physician's assistant who saved my life. I told her about the migraines and how ever since my hysterectomy I'd lost all interest in sex. I felt like everything was sewn shut.*

She said not all estrogen brands react the same way and we finally found one that didn't make my head pound. But she didn't tell me that it also contained a little bit of testosterone. I turned into an animal. I felt like I was twenty years old. I couldn't get enough. Naturally, my husband thought it was him, that he'd become some Don Juan. But it was me. I would be ironing and get the urge and call out, "Oh, sweetheart." I started feeling sorry for teenage boys and how they're always horny. I just wanted it all the time. I even started fantasizing about the bus driver.

I went back to the PA and said, "What have you done to me?" and she told me about the testosterone, and I said we better eliminate that before my husband and I both die of heart attacks. I'm back to normal. My new estrogen pills are fine and I feel as sexy as I did before the hysterectomy. I didn't run away with the bus driver—my husband bought me a new car.

Kate says she's always on the lookout for couples who keep their romance alive:

> *At a wedding reception in Los Angeles, I sat staring at the older couples—the ones in their sixties and seventies who dance and move so perfectly together. You can tell by how they smile and close their eyes or lift their heads back and laugh that they enjoy being in each other's arms and touching each other's skin. If they were anywhere but a dance floor you might blush to watch.*

It's More Than Just Sex

If you listen you may hear a different kind of sex talk. It's not just about who's getting lucky in the bedroom, but also of greater turn-ons. Women talk about becoming more all-around pleasure-loving and sensuous as they get older.

Mimi describes a new kind of awareness that sounds like a combination of religious rapture, artistic sensitivity, and orgasmic delight:

> *I can become fixed on the curve in a tree limb, the feel of my dog's fur, just wanting to touch and rub up against things. I enjoy looking at men's bodies. And women's too. I feel this overwhelming sensuousness that I never felt at age thirty. I think it comes from being menopausal and probably the fact that I'm single and I haven't had a lover for a while. I think women are very aware of sexy and sensual feelings, and we're fooled into denying them because of the myth that only men think about sex. Maybe it's*

*the last rush in the wave of sexuality, but I want
these feelings to stay forever. To feel passion. To
long.*

Sophie took an early retirement from newspaper editing
and reporting to go write a novel in Mexico and thinks this
new freedom to focus on all the senses has to do with timing
and time:

*When we're in our reproducing age, it takes a lot
of energy and focus, but when we're not doing
that anymore, once the eggs get to retire, the
body-mind can put energy into other things. I can
look at small children and just enjoy their
beauty—they don't remind me that laundry or
cooking is waiting. I think some of this has to do
with not having a job to go to—I have time to
enjoy and concentrate on images, colors, tastes,
smells, sounds. In many ways, this age is a lot
more erotic than earlier ages that were focused on
sexuality, in the sense that sensual enjoyment can
be free-floating, not focused on the sexual
characteristics.*

Lily, too, finds the fire burning bright for many things:

*I appreciate moments that I didn't when I was
younger. Sometimes I'm just filled with love or
bliss, and I've felt it enough that I know it comes
again and again. I can feel it just happily playing
with my dog. Or holding my daughter's face and
saying, "I love you." It's an awareness of people
and things that I now do consciously, my form of
spirituality.*

Falling in Love Again

Sam, a business executive with two teenagers, had been divorced for ten years and loved a lot of her single life. But then she began to have yearnings:

> *I like that I can be in bed alone with my dogs and my books. But sometimes I feel lonely. I came home from work one day and someone had moved the garbage pails from the street to behind the house, probably one of the guys painting my house. But just that gesture moved me to tears. It made me think about the partner thing, the dance you do as a couple.*
>
> *Not long after, I fell deeply, suddenly, and magically in love with a man I had dated briefly a year before who reappeared. I'm scared to death because I have so much to lose, and I know that I do much better as a functioning human being when I'm not in love. But given the opportunity, I'll take passion every time. Being loved back at age fifty-three, despite the effects of time and gravity on my scrawny body, feels like a tremendous gift.*

When Sydney started going out with a man after her third divorce she surprised both herself and her mother:

> *I think my mom thought that after three marriages I would stop trying and go into old maid training, and she'd have someone to go on cruises with. I really wasn't looking for anyone and then suddenly I'm dancing in the kitchen with this wonderful man and we're like Meryl Streep and Clint Eastwood in* The Bridges of Madison County. *And he's talking Tolstoy to my*

son and my son is actually talking back. Plus he
likes antiques and dogs. I was a bride again at
fifty-four.

"I think we're just pickier as we get older," said Sue, who after divorcing in her forties from her college sweetheart doesn't have any great desire to get married again:

Maybe I would if I fell madly in love. I think
that is the only way I could stand having
someone around every day. But I enjoy the
continued game. I was on a train in Germany
and met a man I was attracted to and he seemed
quite fascinated with me. He didn't speak English
so we couldn't communicate, but the looks we
gave each other were interesting.

Pam met a man while standing in line at a Costco store:

He was carrying yellow roses, a bottle of wine,
and a box of firewood, and I felt the old
attraction even though I assumed he was buying
all those nice things for his wife. We ended up
talking in the parking lot and he made a point of
saying that he always buys flowers for his
apartment even though he lives alone. We drove
off and then I pulled up at a stop light and he
was right beside me. I rolled down my window
and passed him my business card. We'll see what
happens.

Aileen, who has an at-home business and a daughter who recently moved out, spends a lot of time alone:

I would love to meet someone with his own life.
The ideal for me would be to be with someone
with whom I could come together on weekends

*and do fun things and travel. Then maybe when
we're in our seventies we could move in together.
I meet men on the job, through friends, but I
have high criteria for a relationship. I'd prefer to
love someone and have someone love me, but I
don't want someone who I have to take care of
emotionally. I want a man who is willing to
work on being intimate.*

Ageless Love

The myth of young women throwing themselves at sexy older
men persists, especially among older men, writes Natalie
Angier in her book *Women: An Intimate Geography*. She
muses that women may be attracted to older men because of
their power or money, or possibly because they're more gra-
cious and grateful than the younger, cockier competition.
Angier also makes the point that the combo of old man and
young woman demonstrates the true balance of power in our
culture, which ranks men over women and youth over old.

The Hollywood version—the one that makes so many
of us grumpy—prefers the extreme coupling of old dude with
trophy nymphet, but in real life it can happen that the
woman is actually middle-aged, although forever younger in
at least her partner's eyes.

Lily usually dated only men her age, but at age fifty-one,
she's with a man who is sixty-five, and they've been together
five years:

*I always assumed I'd want to be with someone
with whom I shared the same cultural references,
so I was surprised to find very little evidence of a
generation gap between us. I think the difference
is that he's not stuck in his past. We can talk*

about Janis Joplin and Eric Clapton, but he can also talk to my mother about old movie stars whose names I don't know.

Still, I worried about being with someone that much older than me, that he might develop a health problem and I'd have to take care of him. Then a year after we'd been dating I had a breast cancer scare, and that did it for me. I stopped worrying about him getting old and sickly because I realized there are no guarantees in any relationship about who is going to get sick first. Sometimes, though, I feel more his age than mine, like I might be giving up my fifties because he's in his sixties. I wonder what I would be doing if I was with someone my own age. Would we be doing younger stuff like water skiing? Yet our life suits me. I am more the drink tea, talk, and take walks type. And because he vibrates with energy there's no thought of being with this poor old guy.

Sexual impotence was an issue for us. The first time we went to bed he couldn't get an erection, but I thought, "What amazing control he has, how politically correct he is for not rushing intercourse." My own sexuality went on a back burner while I learned all about the penis and impotence and we tried many things. Finally Viagra worked. That has helped put me back into the picture, because I don't have to just think about his erection all the time when we're making love.

Eve, a college professor, was very young when she met her older man. They were together eighteen years and she says a lot of the attraction was his confidence:

*First, there was an incredible sexual chemistry
between us. I think that chemistry, in part, rested
on his energy, his clarity about who he was and
what work he came to do in the world, his sense
of efficacy and mastery. Those were all qualities I
found, and still find, deeply compelling. I was
seventeen and a freshman in college. We became
friends almost instantly and lovers two years later,
after he left the university. We moved in together
when I was twenty-four. He was diagnosed with
lung cancer when I was forty and died when I
was forty-two. He was sixty-eight.*

*I think I changed more than he did over the
course of the relationship, from a young thing
who relied on his strength to a full partner. I
never felt put in the nymphet role. We had our
share of fights, betrayals, and bad times, but we
always just plain liked talking to each other. We
used to turn off all the lights in the kitchen
except the stove light and sit on the counter with
our backs propped against the cabinets and just
yak the night away.*

The combination of older woman and younger man is
more rare than the reverse, but as Sara Davidson discovered
after writing about her love affair with a younger, less educated man in her book *Cowboy, A Love Story*, there's a definite trend. She told me in an interview that she's met a
growing number of professional women with smiles on their
faces and unlikely partners: "Women come up to me and say
they have a cowboy in their lives. Not the boots and spurs
variety, but a man who is the wrong age, wrong education,
wrong nationality, wrong job. But it works."

Vicky turned fifty the year her husband turned forty.
When they met he was a confirmed loner and Vicky was a

mother and the newly divorced wife of an international lawyer. She knew city glitz and he knew the wilds of Missouri:

> *In my old life I was part of café society, where
> people spent a lot of money and played hard. At
> age forty the curtain lifted. I was living nine
> thousand miles away from the United States with
> two little kids. I said "It's done." With money
> from my divorce settlement I bought a house in
> the Ozarks. I grew up in another part of Missouri
> and knew the place had a rough beauty and a
> rough reputation. I walked into a store and saw
> this man sitting with his feet propped on a wood-
> burning stove and I felt something I hadn't for
> years. He was a self-taught artist who gave
> classes. I pretended I didn't have an art degree so
> I could take one of his classes just to meet him.
> I hadn't had a date in seven years.*
>
> *I kind of worried that he might think I was
> too over the hill. It didn't matter to him. It
> hasn't ever mattered. Now I make fun of the age
> difference and say it just means I'm wiser. I feel
> young but I don't feel his age, because I
> remember how I felt at forty and I'm happier
> now than I was at forty. We traded lives. He's
> never had a chance to paint every day and I've
> never run a store. I write and raise chickens and
> I'm adding a book section to the store. There used
> to be a rule for women that you don't marry men
> younger, shorter, or less educated than you are.
> When I was younger I always wanted the tall,
> good-looking, rich guy but my husband is the
> perfect person for me because he's deep and solid.*

In her midforties, Dawn is with a twenty-five-year-old:

He has an inner wisdom and maturity older than his years. When I met him I thought, "Oh, man, I should think about this," but I was just compelled. Both of us were married before. I have college-aged kids and he has preschoolers, but we both like to cook, hike, and run.

I think a lot of people have misgivings about older women with younger men because women are supposed to be the anchor. We set the mode. It's okay for a man to do something different but not for a woman. Being with a younger man is outside the mode. But society's attitude doesn't affect us as a couple. He has friends who are my age and I have friends who are his age. I don't even think about how old I am.

For Pam it was purely a physical thing with younger men, and she thinks she did it to make up for being so chaste when she was young herself:

The first time I had sex I got pregnant. I went from being a virgin at seventeen to becoming a mother. Then in my thirties I reached a second childhood, and that was part of the allure of young men, those I hadn't gotten to date when I was their age.

Of course, they have legs like tree trunks, which is very appealing, and what they lacked in sexual finesse they made up in enthusiasm. But they also wanted to do stuff—go fishing and hiking, ride motorcycles—that men my age didn't want to do. Men my age often just want to stay home, drink beer, and watch football.

I had a string of young lovers through my forties, including one long affair with this doll-face guy who was twenty-five. He wasn't mentally challenging, but he was fun and he was cute. One of my best friends was a gay man and we'd go out to bars looking for men together. I used to quote Cher, who once said something like, "Have him stripped, washed, and brought to my tent."

Leigh was married and fifty-five. He was single and thirty-two. What first appealed to Leigh, a college professor, was the intellect of her young lover:

He was not only brainy, but also intellectually sophisticated. We talked about everything and would often stay up all night talking and making love. I loved the insight into a younger culture and the new ideas that he gave me. I loved learning more about contemporary theory from him and I loved teaching him how to teach. I liked his sexual stamina. It was, quite frankly, amazing to me, as my husband had never been that way even when we were young.

The worst part was that the age difference bothered him. He was ashamed of being with such an older woman and didn't want to take me around his friends. I've thought a lot about this. First, of course, we had to keep it quiet, so we got used to being a couple alone. But there had to be more than that. Perhaps it was because, despite his sophistication, he was very much a child of his era and insecure about not having a beautiful young woman on his arm.

Being with him did make me feel and look younger. I was and still am inordinately proud of myself for seeing something I wanted and going after it. I made the first move and was really the initiator in most of the relationship. This self-actualization gave me courage to make other changes in my life. We talked from the get-go about it not being permanent. Still, it was very hard for me when he met someone else. There were several years when I couldn't pass a motel without crying. The aliveness I felt in my mind whenever I was with him is perhaps what I miss most now that he's gone.

Will You Still Need Me, Will You Still Feed Me?

According to Kate, married fifteen years to a man six months younger,

I worried more about my husband getting his AARP welcome letter than about me getting mine. Sometimes I think I can handle my own aging as long as it doesn't remind him that he, too, is getting older. I have a friend whose seventy-five-year-old husband had an affair with a younger woman, so my friend went and had a fling with an eighty-year-old man who taught her to cuss in French. I liked her chutzpah, but I don't want to have to be eighty and worrying about my husband's need to feel younger. When my husband suggested I color my hair, I wasn't sure if he thought it would take years off my looks or his.

Kate sought advice from her great-aunt, who believes that women are better at getting older than men:

She said the worst thing for men is when they can't get an erection. She said it's like their best friend has left for Europe. She told me that there are certain things to pay attention to when you're getting older, like eating well and exercising, and then she advised that I just deal with the rest as graciously as possible.

Anne, who is forty-six, says her same-age husband of eighteen years worries more about aging than she does:

To be precise, he worries more about dying than I do. My worries in that regard tend to be about my children (who will care for them, what will their lives be like, how will they get on), while his tend to be more about whether he's sucked the marrow from life and made his mark and used every minute to the fullest. Neither of us worries overly about the cosmetic aspect of aging, which is probably part of why we get on so well. Mind you, we're not above mourning the loss of hair—me—or the decline in muscle tone—him—or the expansion of waistlines—us. Mostly, though, we joke about it. We do get serious about striving for a healthier, less stressful lifestyle and staying in good, if inelegant, shape.

I appreciate that women and men have separate but equal challenges regarding getting older. We have to deal with menopause and worries about breast cancer, but they have to deal with prostate worries and hypertension. As for the wrinkles and sags, there are men who worry about it and there are women who do and there are those of each sex who simply don't. Maybe in some lines of work, aging is not as harsh on men

as it is on women, like in the acting world, but I
suspect you could make a good case for members
of either gender having it harder—or easier.

Goldy and Annascha have been together for twelve
years and are going through middle age and menopause at the
same time. Some of their heterosexual friends assume that it's
easier for two empathetic women to deal with the process
together, to which Goldy answers:

Life is hard. I'm happy that I'm sharing it with
someone. And I don't think getting older is easier
because we're two women, but it does help that
we're compassionate with each other. We do have
separate bodies. There's an ease in talking about
body parts that we have that we might not if we
were with men. If she's having cramps I "get"
what cramps feel like. But my hormone changes
may not be exactly what she's experiencing. I
think as a couple the important thing is to be
sympathetic.

It's also important to me that we remain
alluring to one another. I always want to look
nice so she thinks I'm beautiful. It's important
how she sees me.

Maria, who is ten years older than her husband, says she
was expecting their sexual drive to wane at about the same time:

That was okay with me. I was kinda looking
forward to reading more. But it isn't okay with
him. He doesn't want our sex life to change. To
keep us both happy, we make a date every Friday
for romance. We tell the twenty-one-year-old he
has to be out of the house by 6:30 PM and my
husband and I have an agreement that we won't

argue or talk about our business. I tried red satin sheets. Too hot. But I'm thinking it may be time to try peacock feathers. It's our TGIF. We look forward to it. Sometimes I put on a costume, like a red slip with my rhinestone jewelry, and we dance. That's why the kids have to go. No one is going to dance with you if they think their kids are going to be walking in the room. We also save a part of each vacation for ourselves. Just being in a new place, in a new bed with a view, can get the juices flowing.

Anne says that both she and her husband wear glasses, so they come off when the clothes come off: "We take our glasses off when we have sex. This way we're both blind when we're naked, so no matter how old we get we'll always look the same to each other, in a blurred way."

Adele and Peggy, together for fifteen years and the mothers of two children, are having different reactions to middle age. Peggy says:

I feel like I'm thirty-five. I'm more physically active than ever. I had my eyes done last year, so when I look in a mirror I can't believe I'm forty-eight. My image of forty was being matronly. When I was forty I was pregnant. I play league tennis, I garden, I walk.

Adele says she's tired:

I don't have as much energy as I used to. As a photographer I notice that my eyes aren't as sharp as they were, but at the same time the desire to be successful, in terms of making money and having fame, is not as strong as it used to be, and that's a relief.

Peggy and I want most of the same things in life. The reason I'm with a woman is not so much because of the sexual urge but because my temperament works better with a woman. The two of us talk everything to death. We're very different, but we understand each other, each other's bodies and each other's minds. I think as you get older you know more what you need to have a happy relationship. As for our sex life, there was a period of time when I was not very sexual but now I'm gung ho and it's nice to have it back. Like all couples who have been together for a while, we start to worry when we read some study about how often people have sex. Peggy will say, "Oh god, it's been a week. We better do it."

5

Not Exactly How I Had It Planned

Sometimes I have hot flashes when I'm nursing.

—Lucy

I had a nice, comfortable, goofy life, but it was a disaster in some ways.

—Beth

My husband dropped dead while jogging, so I moved to Florence.

—Belle

I'll Never Become a Foreign Correspondent

In her forties and fifties Leigh's life started shifting. She began and finished a doctoral program, got a full-time faculty position, received a bunch of teaching awards, researched and published a book, ended a marriage, fell in love, opened a shelter for homeless women, lost several friends and family members to cancer, and entered into what she defines as a "new and fruitful, though sometimes thorny, relationship with my children." She says:

> *When I went back to school in my forties, it was exciting to be with people of all ages and stimulating to be in that heady intellectual atmosphere. My closest friend in the program was twenty years younger but we were simpatico politically. Now that I'm sixty-two, I feel like I'm just dipping my toe in the waters of middle age. Getting older has never disappointed me. Even though I'm now going through a lonely time, I wouldn't trade my life for anyone else's and I look forward to what the rest of middle age has to bring me. The last twenty years have truly been the most fun and fulfilling in my life. Yesterday I went through some family pictures and looked at my growing up pictures. I wouldn't go back to those days for the world.*

Our generation of women, blessed by changing times and more life choices than were afforded our mothers, scattered in many brave new directions. The problem with coming to a midlife crossroads, however, is that you realize that with so many roads to take, there were that many roads also not taken.

What's your regret? Kate says:

I've always wished I'd been a hippie, but back in the sixties I stuck with the old pattern. Finish school, get married, go to work, think about buying a house. I became hippie-like on weekends, which was pretty easy to do living on the beach in Southern California. Then I played the straight establishment role during the week, with a job that came with a union contract and a pension plan. I was secure, but I envied the free spirits who followed their hearts, including the women who slept around, lived in a van, and didn't even think about buying insurance. I wished I'd been brave enough to live free at a time when it was so easy to do. I never got to Woodstock.

Now that I'm in my midfifties I can look back on a solid career and a 401K, and my friends who took the wild and crazy route tell me they wish they had some of my security. But I believe they racked up more adventures.

Lily dropped out of graduate school, met a man who invited her to jump on the back of his motorcycle, and took off with him to go live on his grandfather's farm in the Midwest. It was a big detour:

I grew up with the 1950s belief that I'd meet the man I was going to marry in college and we'd move to a small town where I'd become a teacher. Instead I ended up living with an extended family, raising chickens and babies, and making bacon from our own pigs. It was the best

*time. We listened to a lot of bluegrass music. I
had a garden. I felt so useful and fulfilled and
exhausted at the end of the day. But I regret not
picking something I liked in school and sticking
with it.*

*Now that I'm fifty-one I'm not sure what to
do next. I have a job with a nonprofit agency
and while I like my coworkers, I think I need to
look elsewhere. It was really bad a year ago when
I hit fifty. I was frantic, not knowing where to
go, what to do. My second daughter left home
and it's not like I want to do that again,
although I miss her. The feeling is more a
self-imposed pressure to move on, to decide
what's next. If I think about it spiritually, to be
in the moment, my moment is great. I love my
life. But the societal pressure is there asking,
"What's your plan?" I'm not likely to go back to
school, so I hope something unfolds for me. I'm
trying to be aware, to pick up on cues.*

Sissy was a dancer in New York in the Sixties:

*I was very wild. Everybody was wild. I came
from a boarding school, very protective
background and was rebelling from my family. I
had a fantastic time, although it turned out later
that I'm an alcoholic and now have been sixteen
years sober.*

*I was having a great time and then I
developed a debilitating illness that ended my
dancing. I married an actor and we moved to
L.A. for his career, had two children, got divorced.
I supported the kids as a waitress and an artist
model. Before I knew it I was middle-aged and*

not sure what to do next. I was okay with money for a while because of a small inheritance, but I wanted to do something creative. I took a poetry workshop and discovered I could write. Now I'm one of six writers writing plays for a little theater company.

It's a very intellectual group. At first I worried about being the oldest, at fifty-six. The next oldest is thirty-seven. I just assumed the younger ones felt differently toward me, like I was this desperate person in her fifties, but I think I am more aware of the age difference than they are. They seem to love having me around. Now I've sent my picture around to try to get some acting and modeling jobs. I like my photo. I look defiant.

I don't look ancient but I think my selling point is that I don't look young either. I've kind of broken the rule. I'm tired of looking at all the pulled faces and I keep hoping that the time has come where we don't need to pretend we're not getting older. I really am interested in solving this so that people will stop thinking we're throw-aways.

Beth has one of those jobs that people fantasize about doing when they get older: she runs a bed and breakfast in New England. But she has regrets:

I should've planned a career. I never had a decent job. I always found a way to make money, but I didn't stick to a profession and now I wish I had one. I had a nice, comfortable, goofy life, but it was a disaster in some ways.

When Beth reports this, her friends immediately protest that she's very accomplished, she's their Julia Child, her inn is charming, and she creates dazzling dinner parties. They also think she's a skillful writer and should do something more with that talent. Beth isn't convinced. When she was fifty-six she went to graduate school in journalism and began freelancing for newspapers in her area. But when she applied for a staff reporting job at one of them she was turned down, and she's convinced it was ageism:

As soon as the editor saw my face and reacted I knew it was bad. He knew my work and that I could write circles around the twenty-five-year-olds, but I wasn't even considered. Maybe because he thought he'd have to pay me more than an entry-level job, but I was paralyzed by that for a long time. I'm sixty-one and I've missed my productive years, but I know I'll do more. I have more courage now, because I don't care as much, and that's good. Still, I wish someone early on had helped me plan a career.

I Forgot to Have Children

Actually, Penelope didn't forget to have children, she studiously avoided it. Still, she gets the questions:

People ask if I have kids and I say no, and I guess it confuses them. Then they ask what made me decide not to have children. What would they say if I turned that around and asked some parent, "Why in the world did you decide to have children?"

I was the oldest of seven kids and from the age of five to nineteen I was up to my elbows in diapers and baby food. Still, I had this abstract idea that I would follow the prescribed way and by twenty-five finish college, see the world, and be ready to have kids. But I didn't marry until I was thirty-six, and with him the child thing never raised its head. My husband already had two children and when I was around them it was a déjà vu of all the restraints on my childhood.

After my divorce there was a time in my middle forties when I was in love with a man, and right after we broke up I got my period. Well, that's it, I thought. There goes my last opportunity to have that man's child. I realized then I was probably never going to have kids. I have an occasional pang. In the movie The Great Santini *there is a scene between the mother and the son when she is consoling him, and I will never know what that is. I am, however, Aunt Penny to a wonderful young woman, so I get some of it. The man I live with now is younger than me and wants children, and I know that at some point he's going to leave me to do that with a younger woman. I did my child-raising when I was a kid and I did a pretty good job with my brothers and sisters. Now, I'm putting my creativity into writing poetry.*

Adina was married when she was twenty-five and became pregnant soon after but her husband didn't want children and Adina didn't want to be a single mother so she got an abortion. When she was thirty-five and living in a religious commune she had a tubal ligation:

I didn't want to have children because I didn't want to load a child with my stuff. Plus, I had emotional pain from the abortion and didn't want to go through it again. I didn't have little girl dreams about being a mother, but my family was still distressed by my decision. My sister tells everyone she had four children to make up for my choice. I traveled a lot, did odd jobs, lived on a commune in Oregon and an ashram in India. None of it was compatible with motherhood.

I admit when I see a sweet little baby I go a little goo-goo, but three minutes later I'm glad I don't have to change diapers. I think children are incredible teachers. I love holding a baby and smelling the top of its head. You look in their eyes and you really see them. You are meeting another unique human being. But I can have those interactions with other people's babies.

I know that being a woman and choosing to be childless doesn't fit society's norm. It implies an inadequacy. I do think some women are born mothers, are incredible with it, need to be mothers, and should be. But you don't have to be a mother to nurture.

Middle-Aged Mommies

In 1981 when Lucy had her first child she was thirty-seven years old and considered a "geriatric mother." If she'd been fifty-four and a new mother back in 1981 she might have ended up on the cover of the *National Inquirer*, but not in 1998 when the age limits on motherhood were being stretched by medical breakthroughs and the health and will of middle-aged mommies. Lucy's a psychotherapist, college teacher, and mother of a little girl who she had with her second husband:

> *Sometimes when I'm crawling upstairs in the middle of the night, thinking my hip's going out, I think, "Yes, this would be easier if I were younger." But I always wanted a daughter. I had my son and then I got divorced and didn't remarry until five years ago. I was pretty healthy, but I wondered if I could pull off having a baby. I chose a doctor who worked with high-risk pregnancies and whose mothers were an average age of forty-six. My husband had to be convinced, because his son and my son were almost raised and he thought we should enjoy our freedom and travel. We went into counseling and he finally understood how important a baby was to me. Of course, now he's batty about her and says she looks like his mother.*
>
> *My doctor told me I had about a year left on a really good uterus, and I guess he was right, because soon after she was born I went into menopause. Sometimes I have hot flashes at the same time I'm nursing.*
>
> *I know I shocked people. Some of my colleagues asked me point blank, "What do you think you're doing?" To some people having a baby at my age is just too different. When we were waiting in line to board a plane Madeline started playing with my hair and the flight attendant said, "Don't pull Grandma's hair." My husband said, "That would be Mommy's hair."*

Connie was in her early forties when she adopted her daughter:

We arrived at the hospital when she was two hours old. We couldn't make it to the hospital in time to catch her. It's a wonderful experience. The main drawback of having a baby at midlife is the energy thing, but on the positive side, we have more money because we're older and I am more sure about things in life, so mothering has come more easily as a result. When you've waited a long time before having a child, the day-to-day panics are gone.

I own my own business, so I can work out an agreeable schedule—a three-day workweek—but the business does require a lot of focus that I'd prefer to give to my daughter. I feel the tug to work more, and the working world expects you to be there constantly, so I have to fake it a bit. I have a staff, so I don't have to do everything. I don't work weekends.

My husband, who is older and has two grown children as well as grandchildren, was reluctant about having a second family. He was absolute when I met him seventeen years ago that he never wanted to have more children. When I was ready to give up, he said he was ready. Time changes many things.

Frances always knew she wanted children, but she never married and she knew the idea of having a child on her own would offend her parents:

When they died I thought, "What am I doing with my life?" Yes, I have a good job. I'm a teacher. I'm a nurse. That should be enough, but it wasn't. People suggested I go back to school but I already have a master's. I tried real estate. I

*lead a bicycle touring group. I wanted to do
something that would make a difference in some
way. Then, one Saturday while shopping, I
happened upon three different women with
Chinese daughters and decided it was my sign to
adopt. My brother asked me if I knew what I
was getting into, and it did make me think.
Sometimes in a relationship when things would
start to get tough, I'd bale. What scared me
about this was that if I went ahead I couldn't
turn back.*

*My friends were supportive and so was the
national organization that helps Americans adopt
Chinese children from orphanages. I went to
China to get my daughter, who was three years
old. The first three months were really hard. The
next three months were quite hard. It took us a
year to get to know each other.*

*I spoke only a couple of sentences of
Chinese, but a Chinese-speaking friend visited our
home twice a week to help with communication.
We managed. I feel like it's opened my heart.
Friends tell me I'm much softer than I used to be
and that's great. I'm very healthy, but I go to
doctors more than I used to, because I don't
want to get sick. I'm already worried about her
being a teenager, because she already has her own
mind.*

Francis has finished menopause and said her daughter
was confused when she noticed a babysitter wearing a pad
and asked "What's that for?"

*She's definitely keeping me younger. Five years
ago I was pretty bored with skiing. Now we go*

all we can because I appreciate it again, with her.
Having a child brings everything to life. It makes
me more hopeful about the world to be around
my daughter.

Peggy and Adele are both called "Mom" by their two
children. Adele went into menopause in her thirties and never
had children. Peggy, who was in a long-term relationship with
a man before meeting Adele, had never wanted kids.
Together they wanted children. The reaction toward their
decision from Peggy's family was positive: "I told my mother
and my grandfather that I was pregnant, and my grandfather
said, "I'm so happy to be living in this day and age."

Peggy sold her business and became a stay-at-home
mom, volunteering in the classroom and starting a Brownie
troop. Adele is a photographer who sells in galleries in California and New York. They have assigned days each week
when one is in charge of cooking and the other is in charge of
picking up and delivering kids. Adele says:

Sometimes my body is very aware that I am
fifty-three and running after a six-year-old. But I
always wanted children and my family, who
would not have chosen this for my life, has
embraced the kids. My mother loves being a
grandmother.

We Will Not Be Bag Ladies

Ann Richards, the untamed former governor of Texas,
addressed a conference room full of professional women
(including myself) and asked how many worried about
becoming bag ladies. Each of the women, or their employers,
had paid the seventy-five dollar ticket for the day's

conference. None of them appeared to be down to their last pair of panty hose. And yet the majority raised their hands, right along with Richards, who said, "My greatest fear used to be that I would end up pushing a cart full of black plastic bags, muttering to myself." She said she once heard Gloria Steinem admit the same fear, that she, too, might end up old, poor, and on the street. "I thought, 'If Gloria Steinem is worried, it really must be every woman's fear.'"

You can worry about becoming a bag lady even if you have stock options, a partner who promises to be there forever, and a sister with a granny unit. So you give a dollar to the woman with her hand out in front of the post office and tuck away her "God bless you," while you promise yourself to pay more than this month's minimum on your credit cards.

A generation or two ago women didn't have credit cards. Or pension plans or money of their own to worry about mismanaging. Richards and others believe the bag lady fear speaks to women not thinking like economic beings even though half the American work force is female and 80 percent of consumer decisions are made by women.

Richards told the women, "Unless you have money set aside in your own name, you are a fool."

Many in the boomer generation didn't start out making money; in fact, they rebelled against it. Alice is an artist:

> I do what I love, but do I have a savings
> account? No. I'll never be able to retire. I wish
> I'd had a rich husband who left me lots of
> money before I met my current husband, who
> doesn't have any savings either. We joke that we
> should adopt a forty-year-old orphan who's an
> investment banker. I know I can always
> paint—unless I go blind or develop an allergy to
> oil paints. Then I think maybe I could paint even
> if I were blind. And if I developed an allergy I

*could switch to watercolors. But what if my work
goes out of style? My work has always sold, but
I haven't kept any for myself as an investment.*

*I've been caring for my eighty-nine-year-old
mother and my husband also has ill parents. It
scares the shit out of me thinking about who will
take care of us when we're old. That's not the
reason to have kids, and anyhow, I don't think I
could ever have been both an artist and a mother
and done both well. I think about forming a
commune and calling it the old artists club.*

Christine says she and her Wellesley College sisters
trade concerns about getting older when they meet at reun-
ions: "I'd say the most common fears are health issues, retirement, and becoming bag ladies."

Lorrie, who administers a government agency, confessed
she's not a smart money manager, at least not in her personal
life:

*I'd maxed out my credit cards and refinanced my
house five times, but I was ashamed. Women, it
seems, will talk about anything but money. We
all live as if we can afford to have what others
have.*

*I went to a credit counselor to consolidate
my debt, asked my boss for a raise after
discovering I was the lowest-paid department
head, and joined a deferred compensation anti-
bag lady plan to save for retirement. It's like
being born again.*

In the 1990s women-only investment clubs started
springing up, helping to break the gender barrier in the stock
market. Cynthia is president of her investment club, which
was started by two teachers who read the "Beardstown

Ladies" books and decided they knew nothing about money
and wanted to learn. They started out very conservative and
tentative but many have become risk takers.

> *I think a lot of women are racing to catch up*
> *about money. Maybe they felt they would live*
> *forever or could depend on someone else to worry*
> *about it for them. The one good thing about an*
> *investment club is it gets you past your denial.*
> *The goal of the club is not about making money*
> *as much as getting comfortable with money and*
> *taking control of our own. A lot of us grew up*
> *with fathers who were uptight about money, had*
> *Depression memories, and made a good life for*
> *their families. Many mothers didn't work and*
> *when they became widowed or divorced they had*
> *no skills and no money sense. That's not*
> *happening with our generation. We're making*
> *money and finally learning what to do with it.*
> *Our group is starting to act like sophisticated*
> *investors. One of our members just bought a*
> *condo that she'll keep for when she retires.*
>
> *Being smart about money makes you feel like*
> *you're part of things. You're not watching the*
> *market go on and wondering what it's all about.*
> *I just got divorced and I understand bag lady*
> *fears. But handling my money intelligently makes*
> *some of those fears go away. It's a real*
> *confidence booster.*

Mary says she's finally motivated to do some money
planning:

> *I don't want to be poor and have to worry all*
> *the time about paying the property taxes or*
> *getting prescriptions filled and have to get money*

from my daughter. Money is one of the keys to being happy when you're really old, and I'm afraid I won't have much. I'm realizing I should have planned better and not lived so much for the moment.

Sedonia points out:

In the 1960s it was uncool to be interested in money. But had we all been tied into making money, a revolution would not have happened. I enjoyed being part of that and living an untraditional life, but now that I'm sixty-three I'm encouraging my women's circle to invest communally in land. Either that or we can become bag ladies together, using grocery carts from only the most expensive markets.

We Thought We'd Be Together

After a while when people would enviously ask Belle how it was she got to live in Italy she'd answer, "My husband dropped dead while jogging, so I moved to Florence." But that was long after she got used to it.

She was fifty-three and her husband was sixty years old. His after-work routine included going to the gym, where he'd put four miles on the treadmill three times a week:

They called me from the gym and said he had collapsed on the treadmill and been taken to the hospital. He was dead when I got there. That morning I'd told him, "You need a haircut." That was the last thing I said to him.

Everything you read says you shouldn't make a life decision for a year after a spouse dies. But I couldn't stay in my big house. So I said, "I'm going to Italy." We always had a thing for Italy. In another year we were going to take a sabbatical and rent a place in Tuscany. He would have understood and been glad that I could do it.

No one's prepared for something like this. I was a basket case. I guess one of my coping mechanisms is to go away. Three months after he died I rented out my house for enough to cover the mortgage and my girlfriend went over with me and stayed until I got into a Florence apartment. My daughter was away at college and my son was in the Marines. I worried that they would feel like they had lost two parents, but they both wanted me to go. I stayed for six years. Italy was very healing. I'd take long walks and go into a church and cry a lot.

But I was determined to not be lonesome. I decided I had to be open to invitations and life. My Italian neighbor knocked on my door and said she was having tea for some people who spoke English and would I like to come by. I met an American photographer who introduced me to a lot of Americans and Italians. Then I connected with the American Church in Florence and got some part-time work editing an English-language magazine. I took language classes for three months. My friends worried I would never come home. They said, "What if you have grandchildren and you're living in Italy?" and I said, "I guess they'll spend summers with their Italian grandmother." I loved the beauty of Florence, the

*more relaxed lifestyle, the way people love art. I
could walk to my favorite cappuccino place and
they'd hand me my Herald Tribune when I
walked in the door.*

*I made three good women friends and that
made a big difference. Sometimes I had guilt
about loving the place at such a great cost. I
experienced what seemed like a long low-grade
grieving. It lasted for about five years and then I
went to a Buddhist monastery in France for three
weeks. That's when I finally dealt with my loss.*

Belle is now back in San Francisco, in an apartment full
of Italian furniture, working at her old company. Several
things brought her back. Her son was seriously injured and
had to be hospitalized. A long-time friend became ill and
Belle wanted to be near her. And there's a new man, someone
Belle first met in law school in the sixties.

*It was hard to leave Italy but I do belong here.
My life is fuller here. I've had some tragedy but I
feel absolutely blessed.*

Nancy was fifty-six when her husband of thirty years
drowned in the bay in front of their home:

*I'd never considered the likelihood of him dying
before me, because he was actually a year
younger than me. He was a healthy guy and we
had started planning an early retirement. We'd
just bought a condo in Florida.*

*I tend to think of myself not so much as a
widow as I do a single person, my own person.
That's okay. Sometimes I wish I didn't have to
handle it, but I can. It took me a while to get
used to saying "I" instead of "we." You always*

grieve, but it goes from being on your mind all the time to once in a while. The other night my grandson had to go to the emergency room and I thought of my husband and said, "I wish you were here to handle this with me."

One of my biggest adjustments was losing some of my friends along with my husband. It's like you become a social outcast. Other married couples stop inviting you, not just to dinner parties but to large gatherings. Not all of them acted like that, but it surprised me how many did. I'm not sure why that is. Do they see me as a threat? Do I make them feel sad?

At first I got angry, and then I decided to develop friendships with other single women. Weekends were when I felt really lonesome. The first Saturday night that I could take a shower, put something nice on, and go out to dinner with other people was wonderful.

6

Grim
Realities

I was in control of my life, and I want to be in control of my death.

—Michele

It's strong therapy when a friend dies. It puts you in the here and now. It's a good day when you're not driving your friend to chemotherapy or holding her head while she's getting sick.

—Lynn

We filled up the back of my husband's truck and he started off down the road to take it all to storage. I followed in my car, staring the whole time at my dad's reclining chair on top. It was like their life was in the back of a truck being hauled away.

—Sydney

What Are the Odds?

The six friends climbed into a hot tub, a mandatory amenity at their annual getaway at a rented house by the ocean. But one night Jamie made a sober accounting:

> *Out of six of us, only four still had our breasts.*
> *Audrey was the first mastectomy, five years*
> *before, and then it was Ellen. I think we were all*
> *wondering who would be without breasts next*
> *time.*

The women met as young mothers in a suburban neighborhood in the late sixties. Most had moved away, but one weekend every February they gathered to fill each other in on job changes, breakups, children in crisis, affairs, divorces, remarriages, and health worries. In the attentive and generous way of long-time intimates, Jamie said they also observed the physical changes in one another:

> *We've become pretty familiar with each other's*
> *bodies and comfortable looking at each other. It's*
> *different from when you're younger and*
> *embarrassed to look at another woman's naked*
> *body or wanting to look and being afraid to.*
> *We'd long ago voted that Maggie had the greatest*
> *tits and Audrey the best body. One year they*
> *were all very interested in my liposuction scar,*
> *and Victoria came with a scar that wrapped*
> *around her neck like a choker necklace after*
> *thyroid cancer.*
> *Audrey got breast cancer at age forty-eight*
> *and had a double mastectomy, the second one for*
> *preventive reasons. She discovered the small tumor*

herself, seven months after a mammogram showed her to be fine. We were with Audrey in the hot tub right after the mastectomies, before she had reconstruction. Her breasts were gone and there were two diagonal scars. I thought, "Okay, this is what it looks like." Basically, she looked as good as always but she was minus breasts. The next year Audrey came with implants. They don't hang like real breasts and there isn't the same sway and movement, but they looked great in clothes and Audrey had cleavage again. She was happy with them, and we were happy because we knew her prognosis was good.

Five years later Ellen got breast cancer, and her prognosis was not good. When Ellen appeared without breasts it was more of a shock. She had large breasts, and without them she looked very different. Also, we didn't have the same positive feelings we had with Audrey that it was okay, in fact a good thing the breasts were gone, because Ellen's cancer had already advanced.

The next year she was wearing a wig. We were trying to keep it light because Ellen had always been the one with the jokes. She said no way was she getting into the hot tub wearing a wig and made us promise not to laugh if she took it off. Of course when she did we all cracked up and she shouted, "I knew it."

Ellen died two weeks before their February retreat but not before giving her friends one last great Ellen moment. On the afternoon a priest arrived to give her last rites, her friends stood around her bed, even though Ellen was the sole Catholic in the group:

The priest started to pray and suddenly called her by the wrong name. He called her Anna. We all looked up at him and practically shouted "It's Ellen." Without opening her eyes, Ellen lifted her hand and said "Close enough." That's kind of become our code phrase. Anytime we're together and someone screws up we say "Close enough."

It is known as the savage sorority, the sisterhood created by breast cancer. Mary became a reluctant member:

When you hit middle age it seems like cancer is circling the block and getting closer. I had started looking at my poker club and wondering, "Who will be first?" Then it was me. I realized one of the hardest parts about getting cancer was figuring out who to tell and how. The telling becomes almost as important as the thing itself. I didn't want to tell my friends at our Christmas party because that would ruin the party, so I waited until it was over and people were starting to leave. I was lucky. Mine turned out to be something called cystosarcoma phillodes. My doctor called it the good kind of cancer. They took it all out.

Before Angie went into the hospital for a lumpectomy she painted the top half of her body with a colorful beach scene:

I scribbled a note to my doctor over the left healthy breast that said, "Roger, wrong one." I wanted people to know that the person they were working on was a real live woman who loves the beach and palm trees and has a sense of humor.

When Ginger's doctor told her she had breast cancer she was furious:

> *I was the epitome of health, a vegetarian. I eat like a damned saint. Probably everyone says this, but I thought I'd be the last person in the world to get cancer. After the mastectomy I asked the nurse for some of the removed tissue so I could give it a decent burial. It's in my garden, under a hydrangea bush.*

One Last Reminder

Lynn talks about how dealing with the death or serious illness of someone your own age helps to put things in perspective, especially your own life:

> *It's strong therapy when a friend is dying. It puts you in the here and now. It's a good day when you're not driving your friend to chemotherapy or holding her head while she's getting sick.*
>
> *My friend, who had small children the same age as mine, died of an aneurysm on the way to the mall. My son worried that if his friend's mother could die, so could I. He asked me to write down everything I know about him so that if something happened to me the memories wouldn't be lost. I ended up writing a guidebook on what advance information people need to share before they die, because many kids, even fifty-year-old kids, wish their parents had left them more. The day my forty-three-year old friend was diagnosed with multiple sclerosis, I decided I needed to get things done and quit*

*putting them on lists. When my friends got sick it
made me decide to quit bellyaching. I'd say to
myself, "I'm great today. I can get out of my
bed. Not everyone else I know can." We know
our parents will die but when one of our
contemporaries dies it's plain stupid if we don't
learn from it. You say, "I'm going to be a better
person," and then you have to remember that six
months down the road.*

Aileen's older sister died at age forty-nine, when Aileen
was forty-six. Her sister had ovarian cancer. Five years later
Aileen was diagnosed with breast cancer:

*I feel I was given a real second chance and my
sister didn't have that opportunity. I think when
someone dies who is your age you realize that
you are privileged. My sister never got to be fifty,
but I did.*

*My sister's death broke my heart. I cried for
two years. But I learned from it. The whole
experience made me not fear death for myself. I
don't want to die now. I want to be around for
a lot more, but I know there's something after, a
place where our spirits come from. I don't belong
to any religion, but I am spiritual. It's something
I carved out for myself and my sister's death
crystallized it. I miss her so much, but I know
she's fine.*

*I also think that how we die has a very
profound effect on the people we leave. After
being diagnosed with cancer my aunt lived for
two years, writing notes, calling people, sprinkling
love everywhere, something she had never done*

*before. While she lay dying her children came and
sang to her.*

She Was Only Fifty-Two

Michele was fifty-two and had been living with pancreatic
cancer for more than a year. She lived under the redwoods in
what was once a summer cabin, with crystals in the windows
and gold-painted Egyptian gods and goddesses in the living
room. When it came to dying she wanted to do it her way,
says her friend Susan:

> *Michele was done with surgeries and experimental
> medications. She was going to die but she was
> going to stay in charge. She said, "I was in
> control of my life and I want to be in control of
> my death. I'm a Scorpio. We're take-charge
> people."*
>
> *She'd lost forty pounds in less than a year,
> but when she smiled the valleys in her face filled
> out. She had long curly brown hair with gray
> streaks, and she wore purple a lot. Michele and I
> were the same age and we both had grown kids.
> Sitting in her living room and later by her bed I
> learned more than I ever knew about dying. "You
> can see why I would rather die here than in a
> hospital," she'd say and comment on the morning
> light, the smell of her neighbors' wood stoves, the
> fog still sitting in her trees.*
>
> *She took a lot of morphine, but the pain was
> always there, waiting to pounce. She once
> described the pain as "a hot rock that burns
> through me, even into my toes." As she got more
> and more sick and couldn't sleep through the*

*night, she moved into a bed in another room,
which had a TV. It was more convenient that
way and it allowed her husband to sleep. She
said she missed having his arms around her in the
night.*

    *Her casket, a cardboard box lined with
purple silk, sat in the living room for months.
Each time a visitor came Michele invited them to
write something on it, in the same way that
you'd ask someone to sign your cast. Throughout
her dying she was visited by two women with the
Natural Death Care Project, a California
organization that helps people do home-based
funerals. They're like death midwives. Michele
filled out her own death certificate and even
interviewed someone from a crematorium. She
wanted to know how cremation worked and told
the woman she didn't want anyone's left-over
ashes mixed up with hers.*

    *Michele's house started to take on the
appearance of someone going on a trip. Her black
velvet dress, the one she wanted to be laid out
in, was hung on her bedroom wall, and next to
her bed she lined up her favorite jewelry. She
even trained one friend in how to do her eyeliner
and lipstick.*

    *After she died five of us went to her house,
washed and dressed her, talked to her as if she
was still there. Her husband put on her favorite
Leonard Cohen tape and made peppermint tea.
We finished at dawn. Michele's body was
elegantly dressed and her face was soft and lovely.
Her husband looked at her and said, "Isn't it
amazing what happens when you lose the pain?"*

The Parents Are Dying

"I started feeling older when the only time I was seeing old friends was at their parents' funerals," says Alison. "I thought, 'This is what we're going to be doing now.'"

Several months after her mother died, Sydney suddenly broke into tears when she saw an old friend at a summer fair:

> *She knew right away what was wrong with me.*
> *She said, "I think you're scared. I think you're*
> *realizing that you have to grow up." And that*
> *was it exactly. No matter how long your parents*
> *are alive, you're still the kid. When they die you*
> *have to be in control, even if you already have*
> *been in control for a long time. My father died*
> *many years ago, but my mother was around a*
> *long time. When she died I think I was pissed off*
> *at my husband, my son, and my brother because*
> *I felt like I had to take care of them without*
> *having someone to take care of me.*

Alice and her mother didn't have a warm relationship when her mother was well, and it hasn't improved now that she's in a nursing home.

> *When someone dies we like to think that they*
> *turn into a wonderful person, but they are the*
> *same person. I don't resent the care that I'm*
> *giving her now, because she gave me life. I owe*
> *her. I don't like her, but I have loved her.*
>
> *The experience does make me think about*
> *how I don't want to be, though. My mother is*
> *very manipulating and talks like nothing good has*
> *happened to her in the last ten years. She doesn't*
> *like being in a nursing home. She complains that*
> *there are old people sitting around in the living*

room. I look at her and I think that she has willfully made herself more helpless than she needs to be. She was never a positive person. You don't start becoming one at eighty. I don't want to be anything like her. So I watch to see if I am manipulating.

Kate's mother died after having Alzheimer's disease for ten years:

I felt like I lost her long before she died. Still, her death made me feel so alone. My mother always told me I could do anything. She also pampered me and worried about me overextending myself. She was my number one cheerleader and fan. I feel like I have to be that for myself now. My sister will sometimes remind me to slow down. But most of the time I have to be my own voice, which I guess really is my mother's voice.

Sydney says:

I was so conditioned to my mother's criticism that now that she's gone I expect criticism, but it doesn't come. Still, I worry if I'm doing the right thing.

After my mother died I cleaned out the house. We filled up the back of my husband's truck and he started off down the road to take it all to storage. I followed in my car, staring the whole time at my dad's old reclining chair on top. It was like their life was in the back of a truck, being hauled away.

When Jane's father died she inherited a large business with her siblings and a large responsibility. A member of her father's firm reminded her of her duties:

He said, "You have to be the adult now." That
was a dose of reality. I had always maintained
that I didn't have to grow up. Now I'm reassuring
my mother that she is not going to run out of
money and it's me talking to lawyers and
financial people, all the while thinking to myself
that I don't care if something is earning another
fourth of a percentage point.

Rachel's parents died within two years of each other:

My father was my biggest supporter. His actual
death was not as bad for me as his getting
Alzheimer's. When your father has Alzheimer's
you don't get to call him up and tell him you
wrecked the car and have him reassure you that
it wasn't your fault. You don't get to hear on a
regular basis that your little boy, his grandson, is
the greatest, cutest, smartest child in the world.
Just like you were.

When parents die you understand your own mortality
even more sharply and also you reassess your life. Rachel says
her parents had regrets, and she doesn't want to have the same:

I don't want to wake up and be eighty and not
have tried to make my marriage better or enjoy
my work more. When our parents were dying my
brother said, "There's nothing we can do for
them, but we can try to live our lives better."
Their deaths certainly changed my attitude toward
work. I can better ignore the stupid things in the
office, the silliness of bosses, and worrying about
the opinions of people I don't respect.

What's Your Demon?

Whether or not family members and friends have become seriously ill or have died, it's generally at midlife when health worries start to haunt us. We feel more vulnerable, realizing that something is going to some day kill us, and we try to do what we can to stave it off. Rachel's demon is cancer:

My mother died of cancer and it came from smoking. I don't worry specifically about lung cancer because I never smoked, but there seems to be so much cancer around and that is one disease that seems to be so out of your control. I do what I can to be healthy, but I could do more. I eat well, but I stress out and that's not good. My goal is to exercise every day in a way that I enjoy so much that I can't wait to do it, like get up early and go for a run or take a bike ride— more than what I get now, which is thirty minutes three times a week.

I think it's important for my all-around health to diversify in my life, to have more friends, be around more ideas, be with people who have passion in their life. If your knees don't get exercise they calcify—I think that happens the same for your mind and your heart. When my parents died their community was only a couple of people. You could tell by how few sympathy cards we got how alone they had become.

Breast cancer is the health concern in Anne's family:

My grandmother, mother, and sister have had it, so I feel genetically marked. I don't worry about dealing with it myself because none of my family members suffered unduly. My grandmother

*developed breast cancer in her seventies and never
underwent any draconian treatment because breast
cancer usually develops more slowly in older
people. My mother's was caught very early and
she underwent very mild radiation treatments. My
sister had a lumpectomy and chemo, which was
tough, but she got through it in fine fettle.*

*The real nightmare for me is the fear of
leaving my children motherless. My daughter has
severe learning disabilities and is unlikely ever to
make it on her own. The thought of my not
being around to help her at least find a safe
place in her life really scares me. And my son is
ten, at a tender age where he's very mom-
oriented. Losing me would be devastating to him
at this moment.*

Kate is haunted by Alzheimer's, which her mother had:

*The main reason I take estrogen is for the
possibility, which researchers widely disagree on,
that it can stall or maybe even prevent
Alzheimer's. I'm not a pill popper and there are
other risks with estrogen, but the risks are worth
it to me. Basically I'm taking estrogen for
something that hasn't happened but that I know
could be on the other side of the mirror waiting.
Two doctors, both women, agreed with my reason
for taking estrogen and said they'd likely do the
same. I read everything I can on the subject and
believe that one of these days they will find a
cause and a cure. I take vitamin E , lecithin,
Gingko, whatever natural substance someone
believes is good for brain cells. I exercise my
brain by pushing myself to read complicated*

literature and listen to language tapes, and I'm trying very hard to train my brain to meditate.

Sue's big concern is that her body will outlive her mind, which was the case for her mother and grandmother:

I take vitamins and exercise and try to keep my vices to a minimum, but I know that at some point there's nothing you can do to stop the aging process. I just try to live life to the fullest, stay in the present, and have fun.

As we approach the age of menopause, our risk of heart disease and stroke begins to increase and steadily rises with age. Even though surveys show that most women are far more afraid of breast cancer than of cardiovascular disease, more women die from heart disease than breast cancer. Sydney had to do some sleuthing to find out about her family's heart problems before she could fix her own:

Mom had heart problems in her early sixties. She was tired, short of breath, and ended up with a heart bypass and a valve replacement. Two of my uncles died of heart attacks in their fifties and a third one had bypass surgery, but I didn't know about them until I went to a family reunion in Missouri. I reconnected with cousins I hadn't seen since I was about eighteen and all of them at middle age had some sort of serious heart happening. My cousins and I remember our grandmother sitting in her chair a lot and now think that she, too, probably had a bad heart.

When I told my doctor the family history he sent me to a cardiologist who found I had a bad valve that would deteriorate over time and would eventually need to be replaced. My husband at

*the time ridiculed me for being a hypochondriac,
and his reaction to this heart diagnosis was one
of the final straws in the marriage.*

   *My mother died and then my aunt died,
which made me realize time was running out for
me. At the same time I was scared to have
surgery. I was at a conference, actually on my
way to getting an award, and turned a corner to
see a gray-haired woman in a wheelchair who
looked like Mom and my aunt. I ran outside and
started bawling my eyes out—I could see myself
just like them. As time went on and there was
distance between the deaths of those two and my
necessity to address my own heart problem, I
came to grips with my fear.*

Doctors replaced Sydney's aortic valve and she sailed
through recovery, reporting soon after:

*I feel relieved and I feel pretty good. There came
a time when I knew I couldn't wait any longer,
when I began to fear a heart attack more than
having surgery. I couldn't garden for more than
one hour. I went away with some friends for a
weekend and I couldn't keep up. Right after the
surgery I felt my energy come back. The dark
circles under my eyes disappeared. I should have
done it earlier.*

7

Going All
the Way

Telling myself I was going to start painting at fifty made me look at fifty differently. I looked forward to it, knowing that there would be something at that age I would finally get to do.

—Marylu

In another time the single woman was an old maid or a widow who had to go live with whoever in the family would take her in, but I think we can do this together.

—Diana

It will be nice if we don't pass on to our grandchildren a legacy of disappointed women.

—Sara

Who You Calling Invisible?

There is this notion that women disappear as they get older, that they become like the older woman in an Amanda Cross mystery who gets away with the crime because no one paid attention to her. But that could be more wishful thinking on the part of those who don't want the competition. Why else would anyone say that? Is Madeleine Albright invisible? Toni Morrison? Gloria Steinem? The woman next door who is running for state senator?

Merita decided to run for office when she was fifty-one, after her company gave her the choice to relocate, quit, or take an early retirement:

> *Two years before I lost my job my marriage*
> *split up, but I found it scarier to face a future*
> *without a job than without a husband. I was*
> *losing a very livable income and the security it*
> *gave me, and now it was up to me to find a*
> *new way to make a living. I was manager for a*
> *district utility company for eight years and then*
> *new management came in. Had they offered me a*
> *big promotion with a transfer I might have*
> *considered it, but at this point in my life I knew*
> *I was not going to make vice president. My*
> *daughter and I didn't want to leave the area, so I*
> *took an early retirement package that reduced our*
> *income to one-fourth of what we'd been living on.*
>
> *I heard about a recall of one of the county*
> *supervisors and decided I was sort of a political*
> *person, more of a political voyeur, but I know*
> *my community. So I said, "Why not run?" and I*
> *threw my hat into the ring. My sister bought me*

*a book on how to run for public office. The hard
part was running. You have to sell yourself.
Basically you're saying, "Hi, I'm Merita. Can I
grovel for your vote?" My opponents were two
tall, smart, articulate men with very commanding
voices. I was a bit intimidated, but I kept my
focus on who I was, and on candidates' night I
wore my highest heels, a don't-fuck-with-me dress,
and I stood tall. It's easy to say how you dress
shouldn't matter but it does. It shows that you're
serious about what you're doing. I beat those two
intimidating men with room to spare.*

*After two terms as a county supervisor I
decided to run for state senator, but I came in
second as the party nominee. I truly in my heart
thought I was going to win, even though I had
my eyes pretty wide open going into it. I was
embarrassed and I felt I'd let so many people
down. I may try again, but I also like being a
big fish in a small pond. I have no illusions—
when I'm not a supervisor it will be "Merita
who?" But I feel I've found my calling. Every
day excites me. I love being part of the process.*

Marylu made a promise to herself that when she turned
fifty she would become a serious painter.

*Fifty was the demarcation. I knew if I didn't
stick with my commitment I would never do it.
Telling myself I was going to start painting at
fifty made me look at fifty differently. I looked
forward to it, knowing that there would be
something at that age I would finally get to do.*

*I like painting images of women. One of my
favorite models is a middle-aged woman who is*

quite voluptuous. She's been a nude model for most of her adult life and she is completely self-confident. She hides nothing. I find bodies of any age very attractive. I'm curious about them. I notice how faces settle. A lot of my paintings of women are sexy probably because I make up fantasies while I'm painting and I tend to think about sex on a regular basis. Sometimes I'm working something out personally. I love this picture of a pouting woman. It came from a model who walked into the studio complaining about her boyfriend. I told her to hang on to her attitude.

I plan to paint the rest of my life, but there could be limits. I have degenerative arthritis and I can only paint for so long at a stretch without hurting. I'm still in my fifties and sometimes I define myself as old, but I think I'm just practicing, because I don't feel old. Maybe when I turn eighty I'll feel I'm truly old. Then I'll have people wait on me, bring me tea and sherry while I watch pornographic movies.

Numero Uno

Eve attempted to meet men by placing a singles ad in her suburban weekly:

Graduate school happy hour didn't work for me anymore. I wasn't looking for a life partner. I was just thinking maybe sex and a movie. That's not unduly complex. I had ninety responses and went on thirty-five dates in two months, wearing my dating outfit— black sweater, short gold skirt.

I think my problem was I couldn't figure out how to say no. This one guy said that his wife died of cancer, and I felt sympathetic because my husband also died of cancer. I met him at a restaurant for Sunday brunch, thinking "How long can it take to eat French toast?" I asked him when his wife died and he said, "Three weeks ago." I suggested that it might be too soon for him to be dating, and he said that's what all the other women had told him. I'd say out of the thirty-five men I dated there were maybe two who, if I'd had the energy, I might have considered having an affair with.

Sue married right out of college, had two children by twenty-five, hopped around the country with her husband's career, and didn't live alone until she was in her mid-forties. She got a divorce at about the same time she went into menopause, moved from Denver to San Francisco, changed jobs, and bought herself a red sports car.

Men my age disappoint me. I'm very visual. I look at a forty-year-old and I still see myself in that time period. I don't want to be with a fifty-five-year-old, although I'd make an exception for Al Pacino. A friend fixed me up with a man my age and it was clear he was in a midlife frenzy, trying to validate his manhood. The first thing he asked was did I date a lot. I've heard this before. I think what they're getting at is if you don't date a lot something's wrong with you. I told him I stopped doing that in college, now I only go out with people I like. The next time he saw my friend he asked if she knew any thirty-year-olds.

> *I know what I'm looking for, and I can tell*
> *at the first meeting if I'm going to end up being*
> *wild about someone. I really don't "date,"*
> *because I don't like going out with strange men*
> *just to go out. I usually go out with groups of*
> *friends.*
>   *I like my freedom. I can do whatever I want,*
> *whenever I want. I don't have to take care of*
> *anyone else. When I had a family, I did those*
> *"attentive wife and mother" things gladly without*
> *thinking and I loved it. I loved being married,*
> *too. But I didn't realize how exhilarating freedom*
> *is. Sometimes I worry that I won't have anyone*
> *to take care of me when I am old, but women*
> *generally end up taking care of the man and*
> *eventually they're alone anyway.*

At the turn of the twenty-first century the American marriage rate was at its lowest in history, with almost forty-three million single women—more than the entire population of Spain—many of whom were formerly married and are choosing not to do it again. The images of women living alone, which used to center on "poor and pitiful," are changing to that of "self-sufficient and savvy." Surveys showed that women are happier living alone than men, particularly if it's their choice.

But Sedonia believes there still exists "a bias in the culture to the unpartnered":

> *Being single does not make you a lesser person,*
> *but there is still some of that thinking. Single*
> *people don't always get included in couples'*
> *events. People feel threatened by us or they treat*
> *us like failures. I think women need to help each*
> *other affirm their singleness, not be ashamed of*

*it. I say we should start planning ahead to live
together, in a communal way—at the very least
putting our trailers in a circle.*

*I've enjoyed being single, doing my writing
and working on my spiritual life. When you're
alone there's nothing to distract you. The buck
stop rights here. It's bumpy, but you can come to
grips with yourself. I work at home. I have more
alone time than I need. I don't want a partner
and I want my own space. But I want to live
with others now.*

Sedonia's circle talks about buying a piece of land they
can own communally. Her friend Diana, a single mother with
one remaining teenager at home, imagines it this way:

*We would all live separately, but there would be
space for gatherings, maybe a common office
where we could all get our e-mail and people
could have interaction if they wanted it. In
another time the single woman was an old maid
or a widow who had to go live with whoever in
the family would take her in, but I think we can
do this together.*

Patricia, an international nurse whose last assignment
was a refugee camp on the border of Pakistan and Afghani-
stan, said having a partner wouldn't fit with her work now,
which she's found is hard for some people to understand:

*When I went to my high school reunion I was
the only woman there without a partner, and I
couldn't tell if they envied me or felt sorry for
me. When you're fifty and comfortably defining
your life without a partner, you don't get the
cultural support for it you might have when you*

*were younger. Maybe I will want to live with
someone later, but right now I'm looking for role
models, women who are single between the ages of
fifty and seventy who have a great productive life.*

Nancy was in her midfifties when her husband died, and
once she got past the grief and fear she decided to do some
things her way. She started traveling outside the country,
took an early retirement from nursing to begin a small
antique business, started yoga classes, and expanded her circle
of friends past those she and her husband had known as a
couple. She's open to remarrying, but only if someone suits
her new life:

> *Society says men get older and stay more
> attractive than women, but I don't see that. I
> wouldn't want a man my age if he thought I was
> going to take care of him and make sure he
> didn't wear the same sweater three days in a row.
> That part is not appealing. It's nice to feel you
> have a life without a man, because so many
> people in my generation believed you couldn't.
> It's very do-able.*

Sophie lives part of every year in Mexico, where she
says single older women are often looked at with curiosity,
but where she enjoys the quiet:

> *I've always been very fond of a scene near the
> end of "The Lion in Winter," when Eleanor of
> Aquitane is on her barge, heading back to the
> convent where loutish King Henry has planted her
> in her old age—which was probably about
> thirty-five, in those days. She has just spent a
> holiday with him, his young mistress, and their
> dreadful power-mad sons. She has the most*

*serene, contented smile as she's leaving, and I
imagine her thinking, "Peace at last!"*

In My Next Life

At midlife we may have gotten pretty good at what we do but
we don't necessarily want to keep doing it. Okay, got that,
now what?

Iris, a nationally known jewelry designer, and her partner, Elizabeth, who owned a video business, decided it was
time to move on and go live in Mexico:

> *Living in another country had been a lifelong
> dream and at some point in my late forties I
> started feeling like I wanted to be free. First, I
> decided to sell my house, and when my dog died
> I purposely didn't get another. Then I sold my
> business. I was done with it.*
>
> *I wanted another culture. There's too much
> stimulation, too much emphasis on success and
> acquiring things in the U.S. Maybe when you're
> younger you need that stimulation in order to
> push yourself. I didn't want that anymore. Taking
> off like this is something I could never have done
> in my thirties and forties. I couldn't have stepped
> off the grid any sooner. I needed the financial
> security. I needed to be really ready to downsize
> and to simplify.*

Trend spotters see baby boomers starting to move
around and change jobs and locales as they get older, instead
of staying put like most of their parents did. Those who
marched into a career in their twenties while their contemporaries took alternative routes will get to finally be bohemians

if you believe aging experts like Ken Dychtwald, who says it will become normal for fifty-year-olds to go back to school in between jobs and still be trying out new careers in their seventies.

In his books *Age Power* and *Age Wave*, Dychtwald writes about a new "cyclic life" paradigm that has people rotating in and out of school, job, and temporary retirement throughout their lives instead of the old pattern of education first, job second, and leisure last.

This is, of course, music to the ears of those who feel they've met a job plateau, are bored, want something more challenging and a chance to try something different.

Goldy was forty-four when she left the advertising business. She and her partner, Annascha, who's in the medical field, came up with what seemed like a great idea for a web project, but it fizzled for lack of financing. Goldy says they moved ahead:

> *I'd had enough of the corporate world by then and I had some money and confidence, so I wasn't worried. But it did get a little scary when our reserves started going and we were trying to manage on credit cards. Now I do an occasional freelance advertising job, but mostly I stay home and paint. Being an artist is a lonely, solitary discipline, but I'm ready for it. I wouldn't have been when I was younger. Before, I liked the crowds, the camaraderie of my peer group. Working at home demands self-reflection, and before I started painting full time I'd never been alone that much. Now there's no one to turn to and ask, "Do you like it?" Those are things that maturity makes you ready for. To be your own boss, to beat your own drum, to question yourself*

without needing anyone to say, "Work harder,
faster, longer."

Annascha, too, is looking for a break from her health
worker job, which forces her to be on the road a lot:

> *I planted wine grapes in the old horse pasture*
> *and took a class in wine making at the junior*
> *college. I never even liked gardening before, but*
> *I'm in love with growing grapes. I'm trying to*
> *come up with a way to combine my health*
> *professional expertise with the wine industry,*
> *maybe as a health and safety advisor to wineries.*
> *I think it's important not to throw away your*
> *old skills and to use them in the next venue.*

When Sara watches movies that show young families
with little kids, she gets weepy: "It makes me wish I could do
it again, because those were sweet times. I guess the challenge
is to go beyond and do something different and be grateful
you don't have to repeat the stuff you didn't enjoy."

Kathleen pushed past empty-nest syndrome to pursue a
variety of interests:

> *When I was younger, fifty sounded way too old.*
> *But whatever age fifty used to seem like then is*
> *not how I am now. I've started consulting for a*
> *large city museum, teaching part time at a*
> *college, running a focus group at my church, and*
> *recording a CD based on songs I wrote for my*
> *grandson called "Nana's Greatest Hits."*
>
> *This time of life is divine. When I think*
> *maybe I should give something up rather than*
> *take on any more, I remember I still want to*
> *teach tap dancing.*

In her early fifties, after a long career in the corporate world, Aileen chose to start her own public relations business out of her house. It took a push, which she got from beating breast cancer:

> *I think when you get older your risk quotient isn't really high. I know mine wasn't. But when you face death you think, "My God, I better do what I want to be doing." If you're in your fifties you start to think, "Maybe I shouldn't wait."*
>
> *I worked all the time, twelve-hour days, traveling a lot. I live alone, so I didn't have to worry about the impact on a relationship, but I also didn't have the time to even begin a relationship. It was a huge job and I loved it. I was visible and it was ego boosting. People believed I could do everything, and unfortunately I did.*
>
> *The wine industry is one field where the older you are the more they seem to honor your experience. In family-owned businesses you can work as long as you want, but that may change as more wineries are bought up by corporations. Yet, even if a company didn't have a problem hiring me in my fifties, they would expect me to have the enthusiasm and energy of a thirty-year-old, and that I don't have. I don't have this undying drive to work as hard as I can. I like working and I will have to work past sixty-five unless I inherit some money. I want to establish a way I can work at my own pace as long as I want and allow myself to have a life.*

Sam did just the opposite in her midfifties, going up one more rung in the field of corporate communications and moving to a different company:

*They sought me out, but at first I wondered if I
could do it. There was some anxiety, but then I
lucked into a cluster of peers—brilliant writers
and editors who are funny and idiosyncratic. It's
like being at the* New Yorker *must have been in
its heyday. I'm learning from them all the time.*

Now for Something Completely Different

At fifty Patricia took off to work at a refugee camp. She
always wanted to work in a foreign country and after her two
kids were grown, she signed up with an international health
organization that places nurses like Patricia and other medical
professionals. A single mother who worked as a nurse and
moonlighted as a bartender when her kids were young, Patricia still feels guilty about doing this one thing for herself:

> *I can't tell you how many mothers try to guilt
> trip me. They ask how I can leave my children
> and I say I didn't want my mother around me
> all the time when I was twenty-six. I'm Catholic,
> though. If there's anything to feel guilty about, I
> will.*
>
> *When I told some people I was going to
> Pakistan they barely reacted. It was as if I said,
> "I'm going to Ohio." I think it's too abstract for
> them to get, too impossible for them to consider,
> because they wouldn't do it. It's not for everyone.
> It's a solitary life. In some ways it's like being in
> a monastery. But you get such a different
> perspective living in another culture. Before
> Pakistan I was in Africa and I can tell you there*

*isn't all of the aging angst we have here. In
Burundi the life expectancy is forty-six and to
come across an older woman is extremely rare.
The few fifty-year-olds are respected and everyone
in the community listens to them.*

Moving onward doesn't necessarily mean going to the
other side of the world. For Kit it was taking bass guitar lessons in her late fifties:

*My friend who has a band knew I was taking
lessons, and she was pretty sure which chords I
could play, so one night at this Irish saloon she
called me up to the stage. She announced I was
making my public debut. What a thrill. After we
finished three people my age came up and said
seeing me inspired them to go home and get their
old instruments out of the closet.*

Since turning fifty Marilyn has overcome two lifelong
fears.

*I resisted going to Hawaii because I thought it
would be full of yuppies, but I went and ended
up dealing with my fear of water. I was always
afraid to snorkel because if I put that tube in my
mouth I was sure I'd choke and gag and die. But
I didn't gag and die. Instead I saw the most
beautiful underwater world.
     Then I took a part-time teaching job and
that got me over my shyness. It was like I was
a different person. I took control and I was
assertive. I could hardly believe it was me. I
guess that's one good thing about this time of
my life. I've taken little, tiny, exciting steps.*

Mollie, who's been in the theater as a director, writer, and actor, is considering other options as she crosses into her fifties:

> *I've decided either I'll become a bad rock singer or write trashy novels or maybe make a movie. Whatever it is, I'm going to start thinking of the rest of my life as bonus time. I've already accomplished a lot. I've gotten to act in plays that I love. I have two wonderful sons. My husband and I are good friends. I've known some terrific people. That's a lot. I don't have any more goals, so the rest will be an adventure.*

Anne has a vision:

> *I keep thinking my turn will come when I'm in my fifties. Certainly it will be when my children are grown and independent, but my daughter has rather serious learning disabilities and developmental delays, and it's hard for me to judge whether she'll ever be able to live on her own. When or if I finally don't have to worry about homework, education plans, soccer meets, and teenage angst—when the days and the weeks are truly mine—I'm going to sit at my computer and write, write, write, even if it's just letters and journals. I'm going to travel to New Zealand and fish with my husband. I'm going to spend luxurious hours reading without guilt. I'm going to walk all over town, without worrying about getting back on time to meet the school bus.*

Three months on retreat is what Justine, a radio executive, is giving herself:

*I've rented a small house in Santa Fe. I'm only
taking things that delight me. I'm going to write
and work on my body at the spa down the road
that gives senior discounts. I don't know who I'll
be when I come back.*

Has Anyone Seen My Inner Me?

Carole got interested in spirituality when she was fourteen
and thought about becoming a witch:

*I needed to have power. But all through my life
I've looked at different beliefs. I notice I'm not
alone. There seems to be a definite spiritual quest
that is becoming epidemic as we boomers get
older. I've recently been attracted to the Druid
ritual, which celebrates the Earth as sacred, and I
belong to a free-form church in Santa Fe with
rotating ministers. My desire for communion with
the "Divine," if you will, has been my driving
force for years. I think what really clinched it for
me was being in a huge earthquake in the desert
and realizing that nothing was solid and that any
sort of stability was an illusion. It really humbled
me. I think many people grasp for spiritual
nourishment around our age.*

Sedonia, who leads ceremonial circles, says:

*Midlife crises do throw a person into finding
herself. My theory is that our female hormones
serve to keep us focused on other people. They
make us able to be mothers, put ourselves second.*

> *But when their driving force lessens there is an*
> *opportunity for us to discover a deeper and freer*
> *experience of self. I think there's a natural urge*
> *to be reflective and go inward during menopausal*
> *years, but it's at odds with the pressure from*
> *society to be out there and performing.*

Diana is able to go inward in a sacred circle with other women:

> *Being in a circle has taught me to listen and get*
> *deeper with myself. You agree to enter a sacred*
> *time and space and everything is different because*
> *of that. There's space for things to shift. The*
> *sacred is about being in the present, being*
> *connected.*

Faye finds the meditative place in her daily yoga practice. "Going inside and doing the soul work" is what she calls it, and adds, "When you illuminate the inside, it shows on the outside."

For Linda, this inner knowing, what she calls "the mystery and the magic," comes from quietly sitting by herself, interpreting her dreams, and meditating: "All I know is that it's something you can't get at the mall. If I find myself wanting and think I need to go buy something to fill it up, then I get home and sit with myself."

Sukie, who has studied how different world cultures look at the afterlife, tested her own beliefs when she became ill with kidney disease: "It was nice to know that when I was up against it, feeling my death as a very real possibility, I wasn't scared. I have hope that there is more, and that hope made death okay, although not desirable right now."

Novelist Anne Lamott is among those who make even organized religion sound hip. Her version of being a born-again Christian allows her to alternately refer to God as

"She" and "He" and do the blessing at her gay friends' wedding. Lamott says she used to think that belief in Jesus and religion is "not what left-wing intellectuals did," but she ended up writing a bestseller about her own personal faith, practiced not in a redwood grove or sweat lodge, but in a regular-looking church.

Friends Know It All

Four women, members of a book club, friends of long standing, sit in an East Coast living room and Eve says, "If we combined the four of us, we'd be flawless." Like most long-time friends, they are each other's best advocates. When Beth complains about her lack of career the others jump in to list all the other things she excels in. When Anne gripes about her hair, Sam says if she had Anne's hair she'd never have to dye her own. When Sam draws a blank on the name of an ex-boyfriend, Eve fills in and jokes, "She has the sex and we remember it for her."

They range in age from late forties to sixty. Beth, the oldest, says, "I think of everyone over forty as roughly the same age and Anne, the youngest, agrees:

> *Age is not the big separation after forty. After that there seems to be a collapse of differences according to age. The biological and social age has gotten scrambled. You can't define someone by the calendar like you used to. I know people who are fifty who are having their first baby and others the same age who are grandparents.*

In another living room in New England, Jill walks in late, yells "Yippee," makes straight for the White Russians, and squeezes onto the couch. Later, as her group gets into talking about everything from mood swings to dying mothers, Jill says, "These things were taboo all my life and now women in the same room are saying what I've been thinking for thirty years."

In this group of friends, two of the women are retired and two are working. One woman's mother just died and her last child moved out, leaving her for the first time in a house with just her husband. One is a widow, one is divorced, one is living with a long-time partner. Three do yoga. Two play golf.

Nancy, widowed when she was in her midfifties and the matriarch of a large family, says she's not had such a close bond with women friends since she was in nursing school:

> *We keep each other going. One night when there was a big storm warning, a couple of us decided we didn't want to be alone, so we put our dinner together and sat by the fire. When one of the others fractured her wrist and couldn't hold her playing cards with her right hand we all agreed to use our weaker hands. I feel older around my children and grandchildren than I do around my friends. With my friends I feel like I'm always forty-five.*

Rachel's group of California friends includes women whose grandchildren are the same age as Rachel's little boy. Rachel is still trying to identify her first hot flash, while some of the others are on the other side of menopause:

> *It's like being friends with the older girls who told you about having your period. You felt like the baby and then you got your period and you were back on the same page. I'm forty-five and some of them just turned sixty, and I'm thrilled*

to think I'll also be with them when they turn
seventy.

At one of their gatherings the conversation sweeps from a local Superior Court judge race to whether one of them should marry her long-time boyfriend or just keep living with him. Meanwhile two in the corner suddenly decide to give each other makeovers. Pretty soon it's a déjà vu pajama party and the whole group is mugging for photographs with green faces, the results of an herbal mask that one brought in her overnight bag. Maureen, newly divorced and the owner of an Irish bar, sighs, "Women. I am so happy to be around just women."

Old friends become more valuable with each year, forgiving, remembering, anticipating what's next together. Mary, in Detroit, has two poker groups and a book group, whose charter members are friends from an old neighborhood:

My one poker group has moved into a new
phase. After laughing all night about one woman
spilling the coffee grounds, spilling the salad,
spilling and dropping everything, she finally
dropped the birthday cake and we officially
entered the phase of wetting our pants when
laughing. I knew this day would come.

Meanwhile in Savannah, Jane, Kate, and Sydney go for a walk on the beach. One puts in a quick two miles on her pedometer. Another stares dreamily out to sea, and the third hunts up some fishermen to discuss the local catch. They are as contrary in their individual styles as they are fierce in devotion to each other. Together since the late 1960s and their first jobs out of college, they tally seven marriages, four children, and an uncommon number of dogs with clever names. They are two Democrats, one Republican, two managers, one union member, and they live in different regions of the country. Kate says she and her friends expect one day they'll all be sitting on the same porch waiting to be called to dinner:

> *When I'm with my friends I can relax in all*
> *ways. We knew each other's first husbands. We've*
> *drunk with each other's parents. We get each*
> *other's jokes. They were there when my daughter*
> *was born and I always knew they'd make sure*
> *she saw Paris if something happened to me. They*
> *got me through a crazy period. Sometimes I*
> *wonder how close we would become if we just*
> *met today, but this bond goes back thirty years*
> *and it doesn't break.*

Friends Don't Let Friends Wear Knee-Highs

Sydney believes it is incumbent upon friends to keep each other from slipping into a middle-aged rut or appearing in public looking "more hen-like than hip." She and her friends have come up with a list of things that friends don't let friends wear. Others have weighed in:

> *No knee-highs with a dress. No mint green*
> *cruise-style polyester pantsuits or holiday theme*
> *sweaters, especially with attachments that make*
> *noise, such as jingle bells.*

No red, white, and blue makeup, says Maureen, which she defines as "too-red lipstick, too-powdery face, and blue hair." No sausage looks, often caused by stuffing our zaftig selves into our daughters' stretch pants. "Better to err on the side of comfort and go for the old hippie look," says Sissy. No nail decals. "No socks under leggings," says Jane.

No matronly costumes, says Maureen. "If we dressed today like some of our mothers did when they were our age we'd look like drag queens."

Grandmother Stories

Roberta says when her daughter became pregnant friends told her, "Oh, you're too young to be a grandmother." Not at fifty-one, she says:

> *I'm not at all too young. I'm five years older than my grandmother was when I was born. I guess some people associate old age with being a grandparent, but I can't wait for that baby. Besides, grandmothers get respect in my Latino culture, and I look forward to another chance to be with and influence a little child, and to spiritually and emotionally support my daughter.*

Helen Fisher, who wrote, *The First Sex,* says that many anthropologists found the idea that women stop being fertile at a relatively young age for an evolutionary reason: to allow us to take on the role of teacher and nurturer to other women's babies and young children, freeing younger women in the community to have more babies.

Sara's determined to be a different kind of grandmother than the ones she grew up with:

> *My grandparents never touched or hugged or kissed us. They worried we would break stuff and when we went to see them the maid would serve us cookies. My father's parents insisted on being called Mary and Paul, therefore we called them*

nothing. I wrote my grandfather a note when he was eighty-two and I felt silly writing "Dear Paul" so I wrote "Dear Grandpa" and he wrote back that he didn't feel old enough to be called Grandpa.

When my stepdaughter had a baby I felt grandparenthood was a little premature, but there was no way I wasn't going to be called Grandma. It is a change in status, though. I ' wasn't planning on having more children, but it felt like a door closed when I heard myself called Grandma.

Donna had some misgivings:

I had a fleeting fear of being called "grandmother," but there was more to my daughter becoming pregnant than that. She has special needs and I tried steering her in another direction. I called a family meeting and made it clear that I would not pick up the ball if she couldn't handle this baby. I couldn't bear to be a mother again. But she married and is part of a large extended Latino family who give her wonderful support. She lives with her in-laws and two aunts and it works perfectly.

Maria, who belly dances and stands on her head, observes how grandmothers have changed in style and looks in two generations:

My grandmother looked like a grandmother, with gray hair in a little old lady bun, lace-up shoes, no makeup. I don't think moisturizer had been invented then. She thought it was extremely dangerous for a child to skate, ride a bike, or

walk alone to the grocery store. I'm not the
worrier that she was and I don't conform to that
image of grandma. Even though in actual years
I'm older than she was. I love changing diapers
and kissing the perfect feet and round belly.

Carrie gets to play dress up with her grandkids:

I have a huge box of old costume jewelry I've
saved over the years and they go crazy when I
get it out and let them run around the house
covered in rhinestones. One of them told me her
mother won't let her wear her party shoes outside
in the mud and so I bought her party shoes she
can wear anyplace she wants. Neither I nor my
children had grandparents that made them feel
special, and I always felt my kids were cheated of
that experience. More than anything, I want them
to remember they had a fun Oma who loved
them unconditionally.

Having a grandchild makes Robin feel hopeful about the
world:

We had all these worries when we were younger
about nuclear war and all, and having
grandchildren makes me feel like a survivor, that
I've made it. Sometimes I fall asleep lying next to
them, the house is quiet, and I have such a sense
of peace and spaciousness. I can see the future.

Baby boomers are going to create a large population of
grandparents. The Census Bureau even talks about a "great-
grandparent boom" created in 2050 by the survivors of the
baby boom.

Sara hopes her generation of grandmothers will have a
decided impact because of the times they have lived through:

I remember growing up hearing stories about how my grandmother was always bitter because my grandfather forced her to quit her job when they got married. You hear a litany of bad things and it's wearing on a little kid. It will be nice if we don't pass on to our grandchildren a legacy of disappointed women.

8

Looking Up the Road

It's your body that's aging, not you. It's your mind that is the real you.

—Rebecca

At fifty I was still jumping horses and flying spinnakers on racing scows and happily engaged in the negotiations of romance. Golly gee whiz. Fifty and sixty were my best years.

—Susanne

I can't imagine a day when I won't be intense about something. Maybe I'll finally learn physics.

—Helen

Powering On

Rebecca Latimer, who writes about getting older in her book *You're Not Old Until You're 90*, was at a book fair when a woman stopped and stared hard at the title:

> *She told me that she had just turned fifty and that her husband had told her she was as good as finished. He told her she shouldn't wear lipstick and that she should stop dressing like a young woman. I looked up at her and said, "Leave him."*

Rebecca, born in 1905, has four decades on that woman and doesn't stand for anyone thinking they're finished. At ninety-four she said, "This is the best part so far." That was after losing her husband of sixty-nine years, developing macular degeneration, and adjusting to a pacemaker. She's working on a new autobiography, making up for her failing eyesight by enlarging the print on her computer to a thirty-five point font size.

> *My father refused to send me to college because he believed educated women did not make suitable wives. When I was sixty I decided to educate myself because there were many things I didn't know. I didn't have a guru, but I found many guides. From Gurdjieff I learned the practice of doing a difficult thing every day. I meditate and I think it's the keystone to ending up in pretty good shape when you get to be this age. I don't understand anyone who says they don't have fifteen minutes a day to be quiet. Look at me. It must work. It's your body that's*

aging, not you. It's your mind that is the real you.

The best way to fight age discrimination is to refuse to play along. Don't let it be put upon you. When my husband and I were in our seventies we were visiting at our son's house and some of his friends were over and I could tell that some of them didn't expect us to participate. My husband would have sat back and politely listened. But I didn't want to just listen. I had something to say so I jumped into their conversation and said, "I don't agree with you on that." I never stand for not being part of the conversation.

Roberta has a Chilean friend, Maria, who is ninety-two:

She didn't leave Chile until her parents died and she was fifty-five. She became a VISTA worker in New Mexico when she was fifty-six, and at age sixty-two she went to work for Cesar Chavez for more than twelve years. She's so wise, and she's really hip. She lets me know I have another forty years. Half another lifetime. She says she is a different person than when she was young. She says, "Now I am myself."

Nikki, a third generation Japanese-American, grew up in a predominantly white affluent suburb and worked in corporate jobs. Her mother was forced with her parents into a Colorado concentration camp during World War II, went to college in her forties, and started writing books in her fifties. Nikki says:

It's the cultural values instilled by my Nisei parents that have sustained me into middle

*age—my sense of family unity and relationships;
my sense of obligation, hard work, and
responsibility; and my sense of aesthetic beauty.
My own aging has helped me appreciate how
fortunate I've been and has given me the wisdom
to take appropriate responsibility. My husband,
also a Japanese-American, and I are buying a
house with my parents so that we can eventually
live together and care for them when they age. It
means changing our careers and location to be
with them, but for me part of living has always
meant changes, and mostly I think I've not only
survived changes, I've needed them.*

Nikki's mother, Mai, believes that women of color don't
have much time for a midlife worries. Mai says:

*I think of a midlife crisis as looking at yourself
in relationship to the rest of the world and
finding yourself wanting. But for a minority, there
is always the message that something is wanting.
I don't think of where am I in relation to the
world, but of what I still have to do.*

Carol has an older neighbor who gives her inspiration:

*Her name is Mary Lou and she is eighty-two, a
writer, political activist, and minister. She makes
her own clothes, pays her own way, thinks her
own thoughts, stirs things up, stands up for
human rights and the environment. She is a
master calligrapher, very open to alternative
health care, and she just keeps working, moving,
exercising. She never gives up, no matter how bad
she feels.*

Alice has three models for a ripe old age:

Georgia O'Keefe, who said she was going to live her life in the middle of nowhere and did. My environmentalist friend, Helen, who is absolutely single-minded about timber issues. And my Aunt Ida, wife of my favorite uncle, who was the black sheep of the family. She was a nurse in Arizona who devoted her life to inoculating children. She was utterly calm and confident.

And Then What Happens?

One group of friends met in a retirement community. The youngest is seventy and the oldest is eighty-three, and they do not consider themselves old. No, thank you, if the choices are middle-aged or old, these women are holding onto the middle. That is because, as Susanne, seventy-five, explains, the alternative category is not appealing:

Old age to me has nothing to do with years, it is a state of being or condition, without forward motion or passion, a life without throb. Pairing, loving, mating, fertilizing, nurturing, supporting are to me as real and proscribed as breathing and eating, and if you still have the skill and desire to be tight or intimate or attached in some fashion to another being you are not old. That necessary intimacy includes lots of possible partners, among them fellow workers, children, lovers, spouses, friends. When you don't care about or miss that anymore you are walking dead.

As for fear of age fifty, Susanne whoops:

At fifty I was still jumping horses and flying
spinnakers on racing scows and happily engaged
in the negotiations of romance. Golly gee whiz.
Fifty and sixty were my best years. The passion
in my life was in my fifties. I had a horse ranch
in my sixties. Everything on my body worked, I
was still a viable contender in the man/woman
frolic, life was still zinging along. At seventy-five,
lots of things don't work now and I haven't the
flexibility to want a man anymore, so
contentment and cozy pleasures, plus mental
excitement, are the joys of this age. I also feel
like I can't bend anymore just to please someone.
I can't pare away any more from this core.

This group of friends has lived all over the United
States, some in foreign countries. They range in profession
from a White House assistant to a math professor. They now
live in relative comfort but consider it more a reward than a
right. They've had their struggles. Their memories of the
1960s are not as free and tie-dyed as their boomer children's.
Dottie was widowed in the 1960s. Karen was divorced and
had her adopted baby taken away from her because she was a
single mother. Susanne had a hysterectomy, lost her mother,
and got a divorce. "It was a gasser," she says.

They agree that when they were young, seventy seemed
old. "That's because my parents were old at seventy," says
Gwen, who is writing about her Washington career and caring for an ill husband:

Of all the years I best loved my sixties. I felt
better than I did in my whole life. I felt healthy
and strong. We did a lot of traveling. I rode all
over the neighborhood on my bike with no hands.

"I thought of my grandparents as being old in the way of decrepit and crabby, implacable, difficult to be around, negative," says Jerry, "but my mother was young and dynamic for a long time."

When Dorothy was sixty she moved from St. Louis to Santa Fe, leaving behind relatives and friends. "They couldn't believe I was actually leaving. I waited until my father died. In Santa Fe I fell in love and married.

"I didn't like my seventieth birthday," says Dorothy. "I thought of it as a demarcation. "Still, I'd like to live long enough to go into space."

Gwen says, "I read that by 2017 for $100,000 you'll be able to travel in space."

Susanne replies, "That's fine, as long as we make sure there will be four people who can play bridge."

The concept of age definition and expectation has changed during their lifetimes. "I remember when a friend of my mother's died at age forty-four," says Susanne, "and someone said, 'Well, at least she had a long life.'"

Dottie believes, "You're not old as long as you can still flirt." She's been married three times and now has a boyfriend: "I think my children still think of me as if I'm in my forties because I play golf and ski. That has kept me thinking like I'm in my forties."

Susanne was a social worker, ran a dental office, and taught French in a private school:

> But my main job has been making some man happy. If I had it to do over again, I would have lived my life less structured. A charming young psychiatrist from Phoenix wanted me to go to Venice and I didn't. I almost always married the men I went to bed with. I'm not in favor of promiscuity, but I watch women my daughter's

*age and I see it's possible to have a warm
relationship without marriage.*

The women say the key to enjoying life has more to do
with staying healthy than ignoring the calendar. Susanne says:

*I think I will turn the corner to old when I can't
do the things I want. Right now I'm healthy but
I hurt and I can't water ski worth a damn. I've
started working in this program that counsels
children who are wards of the court. I felt I
needed another dimension in my life.*

Karen says:

*I got my Ph.D. and my divorce on the same day.
My husband and I were together seventeen years,
adopted our daughter, and had just adopted a
second baby when he left. The adoption agency
made me give back the baby, who was a year
old, because they had rules against single mothers
adopting. I was thirty-seven when he left. I just
decided to live like I was married. I bought a
house with a pool and traveled with my daughter.
I taught calculus and 99 percent of my students
were men. I got married again at fifty.*

They're sensitive about being treated differently because
of their age. Dottie was surprised on the subway to have a
young man stand up and give her his seat. Susanne says after
a knee injury she needed a wheelchair to get around the airport. "I couldn't stand the pitying looks."

Karen says she was ignored at the supermarket while
younger people were waited on. "I had to wait a long time to
buy fish," she says. The others say, "Speak up next time.
Don't be shy. Make them see you."

Resolutions for the Long Haul

Faye makes birthday resolutions instead of New Year's vows:

*On each birthday I try to reinvent myself. I
narrow down what I want to work on that year.
One time it was working on saying "no" more
often. Or I say this will be my intention this
year, to investigate some field I may want to
pursue when I retire from flying.*

Following Faye's lead, here is a list of resolutions for
birthdays and every milestone moment, which they all should
be after fifty:

*Be nice to yourself. Buy expensive Egyptian
cotton sheets and new hiking boots.*

Stay curious.

Give in to your cravings.

Drive home on the back roads.

Buy some green socks with frogs on them.

*Pass on wisdom. Robin's favorite Buddhist thought
is, "Consider the effect of resentment and
forgiveness; then choose." Neva's is, "Success is
determined by the number of joyful thoughts in
any given day."*

*Buy and use unstintingly the $5 soap that makes
you smell like you. The guests can have the
Ivory.*

*Chill and slice an Asian pear into very thin
portions on an antique plate. Eat slowly.*

Sit in the window, stare at the moon, and spoon Nutella out of a jar.

Avoid envy and bitterness. They freeze on your face.

Wear your silk pajamas outside gardening.

Paint your toenails. Gretchen painted hers yellow and stuck them on her husband's chest. She said, "I like to keep him guessing."

Bloom like the Naked Lady flower. After summer the green leaves go limp and then suddenly there's a single pink beauty standing on tiptoes and waving.

Walk with long steps and lead with your collarbone.

Ditch all underwear that has the tiniest rip, feels tight, or has turned a funny blue in the wash.

Make friends of all ages. Sydney has a photo of herself with her two oldest friends next to one of herself with her two youngest friends.

Treat yourself generously. Mary opts for a facial or a massage, "Someplace where people will be nice to me all day."

Keep learning. "I can't imagine a day when I won't be intense about something," Helen says. "Maybe I'll finally learn physics. Anything that keeps the door open."

Don't believe anyone who says you're too old for dark lipstick, eyeliner, and your favorite black pants with the sequin stars on the hips.

*Celebrate each dramatically different decade.
Penelope went to a friend's sixtieth birthday party
where the celebrant put up photos of all the great
things that happened to her in her fifties—
receiving an award, running a marathon, going to
Russia and Nicaragua.*

*Find a cause and speak up. Activists live long and
loud.*

*Get down with another juicy woman, like Billie
Holiday or Cesaria Evora.*

Do your Kegels. Drink water.

*Refuse to be ignored. Do something outrageous,
bold, unlike yourself. If the bathing suit doesn't
fit, skinny-dip.*

The clock ticketh. To adapt an old philosophy: Today is the
youngest day of the rest of your life.

References

Adams, Alice. 1999. *Second Chances.* New York: Washington Square Press.

Angier, Natalie. 1999. *Woman, An Intimate Geography.* New York: Houghton Mifflin.

Associated Press. 1999. *Study Finds Middle Age Enjoyable.* February 16.

Barry, Kathleen. 1988. *Susan B. Anthony: A Biography of a Singular Feminist.* New York: New York University Press.

Bureau of the Census, U.S. Department of Commerce. September, 1993. *We the American Women.*

Cahill, Sedonia. 1992. *The Ceremonial Circle.* San Francisco: HarperSan Francisco.

Chapman, Robert. 1986. *New Dictionary of American Slang.* New York: Harper and Row.

Chicago Tribune. *Women Seek More Say on Hormones.* November 1999.

Clegg, Eileen, and Susan Swartz. 1998. *Goodbye Good Girl.* Oakland, Calif: New Harbinger.

Dycthwald, Ken. 1999. *Age Power: How the 21ˢᵗ Century Will be Ruled by the New Old.* New York: St. Martin's Press.

———. 1989. *Age Wave: The Challenges and Opportunities of an Aging America.* New York: St. Martin's Press.

Ellman, Mary. 1968. *Thinking about Women.* New York: Harcourt Brace Jovanovich.

Fisher, Helen. 1999. *The First Sex.* New York: Random House.

Friedan, Betty. 2000. *Life So Far.* New York: Simon and Schuster.

Gaitskill, Mary. 1999. *Alice Adams* (Obituary). Salon.com, June 9.

Gordon, Mary. 1999. *Spending: A Utopian Divertimento.* New York: Scribner.

Gray, Francine Du Plessix. 1996. *The Third Age. New Yorker,* February 26.

Gray, John. 1997. *Learning the New Intimacy,* an essay in *Are You Old Enough to Read This Book? Reflections on Mid-life.* Pleasantville, New York: Readers Digest /New Choices Book.

Health Magazine. 2000. *Vital Statistics* January/February, 22.

Japenga, Ann. 1999. "Strong Woman," an interview with fitness author Jan Todd. *Health Magazine,* November/December ,136.

Kalb, Claudia. 1999. "Our Quest to be Perfect," a report on cosmetic surgery. *Newsweek,* August 9.

Kelch, Deborah Reidy. 1998. *Women Aging Well.* California Center for Health Improvement report, October.

Latimer, Rebecca. 1997. *You're Not Old Until You're Ninety: Best to Be Prepared, However.* Grass Valley, Calif.: Blue Dolphin.

LaBelle, Patti. 1996. *Don't Block the Blessings: Revelations of a Lifetime.* New York: Putnam.

Lattier, Carolyn. 1998. *Breasts, the Women's Perspective on an American Obsession.* Binghamton, New York: Harrington Park Press.

Love, Susan. 1997. *Dr. Susan Love's Hormone Book.* New York: Random House.

McCabe, Charles. 1980. "Women Over 40." *San Francisco Chronicle,* October 3.

McPhelimy, Lynn. 1997. *In the Checklist of Life.* Rockfall, Conn.: AAIP Publishing.

Mulligan, Kate. 1996. "Heilbrunian Adventures," interview with Carolyn Heilbrun. Washington, D.C.: *AARP Bulletin.*

Nelson, Miriam E. 1997. *Strong Women Stay Young.* New York: Bantam Books

Northrup, Christiane. 1998. *Women's Bodies, Women's Wisdom.* New York: Bantam Books.

Ojeda, Linda. 2000. *Menopause Without Medicine.* New York: Hunter House.

Popcorn, Faith. 1996. *Clicking.* New York: Harper Collins.

Reuters News Service. 1999. "Report on Percentage of Single Households in Various Countries," October 7.

Sheehy, Gail. 1995. *New Passages: Mapping Your Life Across Time.* New York: Random House.

Snyderman, Nancy. 1996. *Dr. Nancy Snyderman's Guide to Good Health for Women over Forty.* New York: Harcourt Brace.

Wolf, Naomi. 1991. *The Beauty Myth.* New York: William Morrow and Company.

Women's Health Advocate. 1997. "Body as Battlefield," an interview with Carol Munter, December.

More Women Talk About Titles

THE CONSCIOUS BRIDE

A diverse group of brides share their true feelings and offer welcome acknowledgment of the many issues that can make an enagement a roller coaster of emotional ups and downs.

Item CB $12.95

UNDER HER WING

Dozens of women who have enjoyed a mentor-protégé relationship help you get beyond fears that have kept you from reaching out to other women and initiate and maintain a successful mentoring relationship.

Item WING $13.95

AFTER THE BREAKUP

Straight, lesbian, and bisexual women of all ages speak out about what really happens when couplehood ends and offer fresh perspectives on how to rebuild your identity and enjoy a life filled with new possibilities.

Item ATB $13.95

FACING 30

A diverse group of women who are either teetering on the brink of 30 or have made it past the big day talk about careers, relationships, the inevitable kid question, and dashed dreams.

Item F30 $12.95

CLAIMING YOUR CREATIVE SELF

Shares the inspiring stories of women who were able to keep in touch with their creative spirit and let it lead them to a place in their lives where something truly magical is taking place.

Item CYCS $15.95

GOODBYE GOOD GIRL

Dozens of women confirm that it may be scary to challenge the rules that dictate what a woman can be and do, but the results can be astonishing, inspiring, and well worth the struggle.

Item GGG $12.95

Call **toll-free 1-800-748-6273** to order. Have your Visa or Mastercard number ready. Or send a check for the titles you want to New Harbinger Publications, 5674 Shattuck Avenue, Oakland, CA 94609. Include $3.80 for the first book and 75¢ for each additional book to cover shipping and handling. (California residents please include appropriate sales tax.) Allow four to six weeks for delivery.

Prices subject to change without notice.

Some Other New Harbinger Self-Help Titles